Snorkel Hawai'i

The Big Island

Guide to the Underwater World of Hawai'i • Judy and Mel Malinowski

Snorkel Hawaii The Big Island
Guide to the Underwater World of Hawaii

Second Edition © 2002 by Judy and Mel Malinowski

Published by: Indigo Publications
920 Los Robles Avenue
Palo Alto, CA 94306 USA

SAN 298-9921
Publisher's symbol: Indigo CA

Printed in Hong Kong by C & C Offset Printing Co., Inc.

About the cover:

Camille Young painted a colorful Picasso Triggerfish in watercolor especially for our cover. A graduate of the University of Hawai'i at O'ahu, she now lives in Moraga, California.

Dave Barry is renowned for his humorous essays and books. His love of the underwater world brings a special eloquence to these passages.

Quotes from "Blub Story", Tropic Magazine, © Dave Barry 1989.

Mahalo to the kind residents of Hawai'i, the ever-friendly Hawai'ian State Libraries, Marta Jorasch, and our many friends and acquaintances on the Big Island for their suggestions and assistance.

ISBN 0-9646680-68
Library of Congress Catalog Card Number: 2002102727

Contents

'Upolu Point

Kapa'a
Mahukona
Lapakahi Park

Hawi

Keokea
Pololu Bay

250

NORTH
KOHALA

270

▲5480'

Kakuihaele

Waipi'o
Valley

240

19

Honoka'a

Spencer Park
Mauna Kea
Puako

Mauna Lani

Anaeho'omalu

Kiholo Bay

SOUTH
KOHALA

Waimea

HAN

Waikoloa
Village

190

200

19

Belt Road

Saddle Rd.

4WD

Kekaha Kai Park

Keahole Airport

Honokohau Harbor

NORTH
KONA

▲ 8271'
Hualalai

military
reservation

Kailua-Kona

Kailua Bay
Kahalu'u Beach
Keauhou Bay

Kealakekua
Captain Cook

Kealakekua Bay

Pu'uhonua O Honaunau

Ho'okena

11

SOUTH
KONA

▲
Mauna Loa
13,677'

Belt Road

KA'U

Miloli'i

Ninole

Manuka Park

Punalu'

11

Whittingto

Mahana Bay

Ka Lae
(South Point)

4

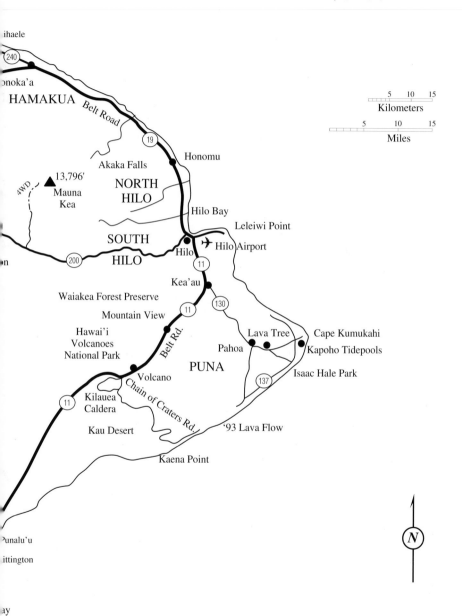

ihaele

240

ɔnoka'a

HAMAKUA
Belt Road

19

Akaka Falls

Honomu

4WD

▲ 13,796'
Mauna
Kea

NORTH
HILO

Hilo Bay

Leleiwi Point

SOUTH
HILO

200

Hilo

Hilo Airport

Kea'au

11

Waiakea Forest Preserve

Mountain View

130

11

Hawai'i
Volcanoes
National Park

Belt Rd.

Lava Tree

Cape Kumukahi

Pahoa

Kapoho Tidepools

PUNA

Volcano

137

Isaac Hale Park

11

Kilauea
Caldera

Chain of Craters Rd.

Kau Desert

'93 Lava Flow

Kaena Point

Punalu'u

.ittington

ay

5   10   15
Kilometers

5   10   15
Miles

N

5

For our young water sprites
Sophia, Ethan and Olivia Jorasch:
a treasure map to the underwater
world of the Big Island of Hawai'i

Why Snorkel the Big Island?

We came from the sea. Our blood is salty, as are our tears. Many years have passed since our primitive ancestors left the sea, yet the water still beckons in our dreams. Snorkeling allows us to follow those dreams and enjoy the most colorful show on earth.

When you don that mask and snorkel, and gently place your face toward the sea, you've entered another planet—one completely unlike home. Everything works differently here in the sea. It's graceful, soft and inviting, with a dazzling array of color and whimsical life forms.

Scuba, with its elaborate, expensive equipment, is one way to enter this world. Snorkeling is a lighter, easier way, a family sport, available to all ages and abilities. Once you've arrived in Hawai'i, it's a remarkable bargain—the best in the islands.

The Big Island offers some of the clearest water and finest sites in all the Hawai'ian islands. Less developed than Maui and O'ahu, it retains much of the aloha spirit. Most kama'aina are friendly, relaxed and willing to share their love of this remarkable island.

Snorkel Hawai'i: The Big Island makes it easy

We've done extensive research that will help you quickly locate appropriate sites to fit your interests and abilities, saving your valuable vacation hours.

Snorkeling sites in Hawai'i are sometimes tricky because of changeable waves and currents, so it's best to get good advice before heading out. Everyone has had their share of unpleasant experiences due to vague directions as well as outdated or inaccurate information. We have created the Snorkel Hawai'i series as that savvy snorkeling buddy everyone needs. We've included many personal stories; see About the Authors on page 192 if you want to know a little more about us.

We have snorkeled all the major sites many times. The challenge lies in finding them quickly, knowing how to enter and exit, and deciding where to snorkel, so you'll have a safe and rewarding experience. Our detailed maps and instructions will guide you to all the best snorkeling, saving you valuable time and effort.

Try to visit The Big Island at least once in your life and by all means don't miss the underwater world. Aloha!

—Judy and Mel Malinowski

Snorkeling is...

- easy
- relaxing
- fun
- easier to learn than swimming
- floating on the surface of the sea
- open to any age, size, shape or ability
- breathing without effort through a tube
- peering into the water world through a mask

Who was the first snorkeler? As the fossil records include few petrified snorkels, we are free to speculate.

Among larger creatures, elephants are the pioneers and current champions, as they have known how to snorkel for countless generations. Once in a blue moon, you may see a elephant herd heading out to do lunch on an island off the coast of Tanzania, paddling along with their trunks held high. No one knows whether the hefty pachyderms enjoy the fish-watching, but you can bet a big liquid chuckle reverberates through the ranks of reef fish in the vicinity as the parade goes by.

As evolution continued, perhaps a clever member of the promising homo sapiens species saved his furry brow by hiding underwater from pursuers, breathing through a hollow reed. Masks came much later, so the fish probably looked a little fuzzy. Surviving to propagate his brainy kind, he founded a dynasty of snorkelers. Perhaps he actually liked the peaceful atmosphere down there, and a new sport was born.

Some of our readers may grumble that snorkeling is not a real sport: no rules, no score, no competition, scarcely aerobic, with hardly any equipment or clothing. We say to them: lighten up, you're on vacation!! Go for a long run later.

Incorrigible competitors can create their own competition by counting how many species they've seen or trying to spot the biggest or the most seen in one day. Everybody else can relax and just have fun being a part of nature's colorful, salty, wet, ancient home.

Basics

To snorkel you need only two things:

Snorkel   Saves lifting your head once a minute, wasting
              energy and disturbing the fish.

Mask   While you can see (poorly) without one, it keeps the
              water out of your eyes and lets you see clearly.

Rent them inexpensively at many local shops or buy them if you
prefer. It's all the back-to-basics folks need to snorkel in calm warm
water, where there aren't any currents or hazards.

Savvy snorkelers often add a few items to the list, based on years of
experience, such as:

Swimsuit   Required by law in many localities. Added benefit:
              can save you from an occasional all-body sunburn.

Fins   Good if you want to swim with ease and speed like
              a fish. Saves energy. A must in Hawai'i, due to
              occasional strong currents. They protect your
              tender feet too.

T-shirt   Simple way to avoid or minimize sunburn on your
              back. Available everywhere.

Sunscreen   To slather on the tender exposed backside skin of
              your legs, neck, and the backs of your arms. Not
              optional in Hawai'i for light-skinned snorkelers.

Lycra Skin   A great all-body coverup for warm weather.
              Provides much better protection than a T-shirt, and
              saves gallons of sunscreen.

Wetsuit   For some, the Hawai'ian waters seem a bit chilly—
              not exactly pool-warm. Wetsuits range from simple
              T-shirt-like tops to full suits. Worth considering.
              Fringe benefit: free sun protection!

You're almost ready to get wet. But wait! You want to know even
more technical detail? Every sport has an equipment list—it's what
keeps sporting goods stores in business and your garage shelves full.

Gear Selection

Good snorkeling gear enables you to pay attention to the fish instead of uncomfortable distractions. Poor equipment will make you suffer in little ways, from pressure headaches caused by a too-tight mask, to blisters on your feet from ill-fitting fins. Consider your alternatives carefully before buying and you'll have more fun later.

Snorkel

Snorkels can be quite cheap. Be prepared to pony up $15 or more if you want them to last awhile and be comfortable. You'll appreciate a comfortable mouthpiece if you plan to snorkel for long. Watch out for hard edges—a good mouthpiece is smooth and chewy-soft. Some of the more expensive mouthpieces swivel for comfort.

Several new high-tech models have been designed to minimize water coming down the tube from chop or an occasional swell over-topping you. We looked at these with mild skepticism until a choppy snorkeling trip had us coughing and clearing our snorkels every third breath. With our new dry snorkels, that water never makes it to the mouthpiece.

Technology continues to advance, so you can now get a snorkel that will keep ALL of the water out—even if you dive beneath the surface. Don't ask us how they do it, but it works well! Even in very choppy conditions, you never worry about water coming in. We like the Ocean Master dry snorkel, starting at $40. It certainly makes learning to snorkel as easy as possible, although is not a necessity.

These fancier snorkels do need care because you won't want a valve to fail just as you arrive at that perfect destination. At least, in Hawai'i, repairs or replacements are usually available.

Snorkel Holder

This little guy holds your snorkel to your mask strap, so you don't keep dipping it in the sea. The standard is a simple figure 8 double loop that pulls over the snorkel tube, wraps around your mask strap, and then back over the tube. A hefty rubber band will work passably in a pinch.

The higher end snorkels usually have a slot that allows the snorkel to be adjusted easily. It slides rather than having to be tugged. The standard Scuba snorkel position is on your left side. You might as well get used to it there since you may dive eventually.

Mask

Nothing can color your snorkeling experience more than an ill-fitting mask. Unless, of course, you get that all-body sunburn mentioned earlier. Don't settle for painful or leaky masks! If it hurts, it's not your problem—it's the mask that's wrong for you. In this case "pain, no gain" applies.

Simple variety store masks can cost as little as $10. Top-quality masks from a dive shop run upwards of $60. Consider starting out with a rental mask, paying a bit extra for the better quality models. As you gain more experience, you'll be in a better position to evaluate a mask before you lock yourself into one style.

You need a good fit to your particular facial geometry. Shops often tell you to place the mask on your face (without the strap) and breathe in. If the mask will stay in place, then they say you have found a good fit. However, nearly all masks will stay on my face under this test, yet some leak later!

Look for soft edges and a mask that conforms to your face even before drawing in your breath. There's a great deal of variance in where a mask rests on your face and how soft it feels, so compare very carefully. Look for soft and comfortable, unless you especially like having pressure headaches and don't mind looking like a very large octopus glommed on to your face.

Lack of 20-20 vision needn't cut into your viewing pleasure, but it does require a little more effort during equipment selection. Those who wear contact lenses can use them within their masks, taking on the risk that they'll swish out and float softly and invisibly down to the sea bed, perhaps to be found by a fossil hunter in the distant future, but certainly not by you. Use the disposable kind. Unless you use contacts, search for a correctable mask. Vision-correcting lens are available for many masks in 1/2 diopter increments.

parrotfish

If the mask you prefer doesn't offer standard correcting lenses, custom prescription lenses can be fitted to almost any mask. This costs more and takes longer. Even bifocals are available. We happen to prefer the comfortable prescription masks made by SeaVision which can be ordered with any custom correction. The cost is much like normal prescription lenses.

Mustaches create a mask leakage problem. As I like the look of a mustache, I have coped with this my entire adult life. Some advise the use petroleum jelly or silicon compound to make a more effective seal. That doesn't appeal to me since I go in and out of the water several times a day. It does help to choose a mask that rests high over the mouth and perhaps trim the top 1/8 inch or so off the center mustache, if it sticks up. Hair breaks the seal and allows water to seep into the mask slowly, so you'll still have to clear the mask occasionally. I've learned to tolerate half an inch of water in the bottom of my mask, though that doesn't work for everyone.

Someone who has struggled with a leaky mask may prefer having a purge valve. There are some clever higher-end purge valve masks. The challenge is how to fit in a purge valve without making it harder to pinch your nose to equalize your ears when surface or scuba diving.

The conventional wisdom in Scuba is that purge valves are an unnecessary weak point. Nevertheless, there are experienced divers who use them. This isn't an issue snorkelers need worry about. If you find a purge valve mask that fits well, use it.

Mask Strap

The strap that comes with the mask is generally fine, but if you have your own mask and want it to slide on more easily, there's a comfortable strap available with adjustment by velcro. The back is made of wetsuit material—stretchy and soft. Cost is about $12 in dive shops. Since we get in and out so often, we happen to prefer this one to the regular strap, but it's a convenience for the frequent snorkeler rather than a necessity.

convict tang

Low Volume Masks

When you begin looking at masks, the variety can be bewildering. How can you figure out which design is best for you?

Inexpensive masks tend to have one large flat front glass. They're OK if the skirt of the mask fits you, although they're often a bit stiff and uncomfortable. They also tend to be far out from your face with a big air space. As you go up in price, the lenses tend to get smaller and closer to your eyes, as preferred by divers.

There is a good Scuba reason for this. These are called "low volume" masks. They contain less airspace and so require less effort to clear when water gets in. They also press less against your face when you go deeper and the pressure rises (if you forget to blow higher pressure air in through your nose) and hence are more comfortable when diving.

For a snorkeler this is of little importance, but it still should be considered as you select your mask. Many snorkelers go on to do some surface diving, as well as Snuba® or Scuba diving. When you dive down even 10', the water pressure is considerable. At 32', the air in your lungs and mask is compressed to half its volume, and unless you remember to blow some air into your mask through your nose, the pressure on your face can be most uncomfortable!

If your mask is flooded, which does happen occasionally, it is easier to clear out the water from a low volume mask. So, while it's not the most important factor, if everything else is equal, low volume is better.

Fins

The simplest fins are basic (usually black) enclosed foot fins. These are one-piece molded rubber and slip right on to your bare feet. For warm water, basic snorkeling, these inexpensive fins are fine. We own several kinds of fins and still often choose the one-piece foot fins for lightness and compact packing. They seem to last forever and are inexpensive ($15-$25).

Why should anyone look further? Because it is possible to get better comfort and more thrust. Specialized fins are now made for higher performance. We tested three sets of fins, doing timed swims over a measured course. The basic fins discussed above went first. A set of fairly expensive, but rather soft, flexible strap-on fins cut the swim time by 20%, while ultra long, stiff-bladed foot-mount Cressi fins cut it by 40%! These long surface diving fins are, however, a little long and awkward to use for most surface snorkeling.

Opinions vary about the merits of flexible fin blades versus stiff blades. We've tested both for snorkeling, and we prefer light, thin, stiff blades, hands down. We also prefer fins that don't float, which isn't an issue with Scuba divers, but can reduce a snorkeler's efficiency if it holds the fins too high in the water.

Our current favorites are Oceanic Vortex fins, with a very comfortable molded shoe and split blades. They feel good on your bare feet, and seem to give you lots of speed for less effort.

You're better off with a medium blade foot fin for most snorkeling. Large diving fins are awkward for snorkeling, and require more leg strength than most non-athletes possess. The big diving fins do come in numerous shapes and colors, which some people are convinced will make them faster or perhaps more attractive. Speed is not the main aim of snorkeling, but has its uses. Faster fins do enable you to cover more territory and they also serve as excellent insurance in case you wander into a strong current. Unless it's absolutely certain that no current can carry you away, ALWAYS WEAR FINS!

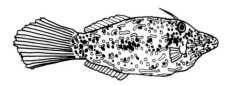

scrawled filefish

14

As you look at more advanced fins, they split into two attachment methods with pros and cons to each type. We own both and pick the best for a particular situation.

ENCLOSED FOOT | Your bare foot slides into a stretchy, integral molded rubber shoe.

Advantages | The lightest, most streamlined and fish-like fit. It probably is the most efficient at transmitting your muscle power to the blade. We prefer this type when booties are not required for warmth or safety.

Disadvantages | The fins must be closely fitted to your particular foot size. Some models may cause blisters. If you have to hike in to the entry site, you need separate shoes. This may preclude entering at one spot, and exiting elsewhere. If you hike over rough ground (a'a lava, for example) to get to your entry point, or the entry is over sharp coral or other hazards, these may not be the best choice.

STRAP-ON | Made for use with booties.

Advantages | Makes rough surface entry easy. Just hike to the entry point, head on into the water holding your fins in hand, lay back and pull on your fins. Exiting is just as easy. The bootie cushions your foot, making blisters unlikely. Widely used for Scuba.

Disadvantages | Less streamlined. The bootie makes your feet float up, so you may have trouble keeping your fins from breaking the surface.

No matter how good the fins, snorkeling for long hours may cause blisters—especially on the heel. No need to worry if you carry 3M Nexcare waterproof bandages. These little essentials will do the job and stay in place well when wet. Buy them at a major pharmacy before your trip—they can be hard to find in the islands.

Reef Shoes or Booties

Walking with bare feet on a'a (sharp lava) or coral can shred your feet in a quick minute. There are fine reef shoes available that are happy in or out of the water. These are primarily for getting there, or wading around, as they don't really work that well with strap-on fins. For the sake of the reef, don't actually walk on a reef with reef shoes, since each step kills hundreds of the little animals that make up the living reef.

Zip-on booties are widely used by divers and allow use of strap-on fins. They do float your feet—a disadvantage for snorkelers.

Keeping Time

One easy-to-forget item: a water-resistant watch. This needn't be expensive and is very useful for pacing yourself and keeping track of your sun exposure time.

"Water resistant" alone usually means that a little rain won't wreck the watch, but immersion in water may. When a designation like "to 10 meters" is added, it denotes added water-resistance; but the dynamic pressures from swimming increase the pressure, so choose 50 meters or greater rating to be safe even when snorkeling. Don't take a 50 meter watch Scuba diving, though—that requires 100-200 meter models.

Hawai'ian time is two hours earlier than Pacific Standard Time or three hours earlier than Pacific Daylight Time. Hawai'i doesn't observe Daylight Savings Time.

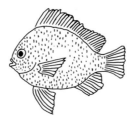

Hawai'ian damselfish

Body Suit

There are a variety of all-body suits that protect you from sun exposure and light abrasion, but provide no warmth. They are made from various synthetic fabrics—lycra and nylon being common. They cost much less than wetsuits and are light and easy to pack. We usually bring ours along as a sun protection alternative in warmer conditions. If you don't want to look like a F.O.B. (Fresh Off the Boat) tourist, with a shocking pink outline of your swimsuit, plan ahead about sun protection. You'll sleep better if you do too. And the fish will not miss all that sunscreen fouling their water.

Wetsuit

In Hawai'i, average water temperature on the surface varies from a low of about 72° F in March to a high of about 80° F in September. If you happen to be slender, no longer young or from a moderate climate, this can seem cold. Sheltered bays and tidepools can be a bit warmer while deeper water can be surprisingly cold. Fresh water runoff can also make water cooler than you might expect. We've snorkeled in March when we swore it was not above 65° F off Kaua'i.

Regardless of the exact temperature, the water is cooler than your body. With normal exertion, your body still cools bit by bit. After awhile, perhaps 30-45 minutes, you start feeling a little chilly. Later you begin shivering and eventually hypothermia begins.

We like to snorkel for two or more hours sometimes. A thin wetsuit protects us from the sun while keeping us warm and comfortable. Off the rack suits are a bargain and fit most folks. Look for a snug fit at neck, wrists and ankles—if your suit is loose there, water will flow in and out, making you cold. If you have big feet and small ankles, get zippers on the legs if possible or you'll really have to struggle to remove the suit when it's wet.

Wetsuit wearers get added range and buoyancy. Wetsuit wearers hardly need a life jacket! Wearing a wetsuit, you can stay in the water without hypothermia for many hours—even in the winter. This could be comforting in the unlikely event that some strong current sweeps you off towards Fiji. There are few situations from which you can't rescue yourself if you're wearing a wetsuit and fins.

We recently discovered a new technology we like a lot: Henderson Gold Core wetsuits, made in Millville, New Jersey. The inside of this suit is coated with a gold-colored nylon that slides on like a breeze wet or dry, and the inner surface dries very quickly. The three millimeter-thick version is light, warm enough for Hawai'i snorkeling and has extra stretch so it's comfortable and easy to get on and off.

Even Gold Core slides poorly on skin with dried on sticky saltwater (as when you're getting in and out frequently on a multi-stop boat trip), though better than regular wetsuits. We found, however, that if you get wet first (in a beach shower, boat shower, or jumping in), Gold Core slides on like teflon.

Dave Barry once described putting on a wetsuit as like wrestling with an octopus. Not this one! No more hanging onto the shower while your buddy tries to pull the wetsuit off your ankles with a winch. If you can afford the extra cost, the suit is superb. We had ours custom-made with longer arms and legs, and no rubberized kneepads. We like our wetsuits sleek and flexible.

Swim Cap

If you have trouble with long hair tangling in your mask straps while snorkeling, get a lycra Speedo swim cap. It may look silly, but it works, and also protects your scalp from too many rays.

Snorkeling Vest

It is possible to buy inflatable vests made for snorkeling. Some guidebooks and stores promote them as virtually essential. We've taken excursions that require all snorkelers to wear one. Other excursions encourage the use of floatation "noodles" or kick boards—whatever it takes to make you comfortable.

Vests are hardly necessary in salt water for most people, but can be useful if you can't swim a lick or won't be willing to try this sport without it. There is a possible safety edge for kids or older folks. If you do get a vest, you can give it to another beginner after you get used to snorkeling. You will discover that it takes little effort to float flat in the water while breathing through a snorkel.

If you want extra flotation, consider using a light wetsuit instead. It simultaneously gives you buoyancy, sun and critter protection, and warmth.

There is a great resource available on all the islands—one of the best bargains in Hawai'i.

For just $25, any Hawai'ian library will issue you a library card good for three years. This gives you full access to the rich and varied collections in the many local libraries. Believe us, if you take advantage of this, you'll be glad you did.

We make a stop at our local library soon after we arrive, checking out books on natural history, fish identification, Hawai'ian history and language, and much more. The "Hawai'iana" section in each library is a collection of books that include the above topics, and a good place to start.

You can check out a full range of videos for a week for just $1 each (one of the few things that cost extra). Don't forget to try some music CDs or tapes, too. If you're interested, you can look over USGS topographic maps. Copy machines are available at ten cents per page.

All the libraries have internet terminals, and you can reserve an hour's session for free (though the sessions can be booked long in advance). You must hold a library card to use the internet. Sometimes, you can pick up a quick ten minutes if the terminal is free between sessions. Pick up your email and browse the web. Or sit in comfortable chairs and read an assortment of local newspapers and magazines. Take a relaxing break in the hospitable libraries of Hawai'i.

Surface Diving Gear

For surface diving, bigger fins help your range. Those surreal-looking Cressi fins that seem about three feet long will take you down so fast you'll be amazed. You'll also be amazed how few suitcases are wide enough to accommodate them.

A long-fin alternative is to use a soft weight belt with from 2 to 4 pounds (more if you wear a wetsuit)—just enough to help you get under the surface without using up all your energy. As you descend, you become neutrally buoyant at about 15-20 feet so you don't have to fight popping up. Of course, the sword cuts two ways, since you must swim up under your own power in time to breathe.

Into the Water

Getting Started

Now that you've assembled a nice collection of snorkel gear, you're ready to go! On a sunny tropical morning you're down at the water's edge. Little one-foot waves slap the sand lightly, while a soft warm breeze takes the edge off the intensity of the climbing sun. It's a great day to be alive and out in the water.

Going snorkeling, it's better to have no suntan lotion on your face or hands. You sure don't want it washing into your eyes to make them burn and water. Wear a nice big hat instead. You applied lotion to your back before you left, so it had time to become effective. Then you washed off your hands and rinsed them well so the lotion couldn't contaminate your mask later.

Or you could do like we do, and skip all the lotion. Being outside as much as we are, and in and out of the water, we prefer to carefully cover up instead—we find too much lotion hard on our skin. Big broad hats like your boat captain wears help. Comfortable cotton cover-ups look good and are cool. Lycra body suits or wetsuits in the water let you stay in for as long as you wish. Do watch out for reflected light on long boat trips, which can sneak in and sizzle your tender face.

Checking Conditions

Take it nice and slow. Sit down and watch the waves for awhile. Check the slope of the beach. Consider whether there might be currents. Look for wave patterns, how big the biggest waves are and how far they wash up on the beach. When you see the pattern, you're ready to go. Set your gear down back well beyond the furthest watermarks on the sand. You don't want that seventh wave to sweep your gear away! Watch as long as it takes to be sure conditions aren't changing for the worse.

Gearing Up

Now defog the mask so that water vapor from your nose, or water leakage, won't bead up on your mask lens and spoil your view. There are two ways to defog.

The classic solution is: SPIT. Spit on the inside of your dry mask lens, and rub it all around with your sunscreen-free finger. Step into the water, just out beyond the stirred up sand, and dip up a mask full of clear saltwater. Thoroughly rub and rinse off that spit, and dump the mask. Now you have prepared a mask that should be fog-resistant for an average snorkel.

If you spit and polish, and still have fogging problems, there are several possible causes. Your mask may be gooped up with cosmetics, dried on saltwater residue or whatever other goo may be out there. A good cleaning with toothpaste may be in order (see Caring for Your Gear, page 25).

It's possible that you didn't actually wet all the surface with spit; perhaps because there were drops of water left on the lens. In that case, or if you just feel funny about spitting in your mask, you can use no-fog solution. No-fog solution for masks actually does work even better than spit. It comes in small, handy, inexpensive bottles that seem to last forever because you use only a few drops at a time. If you prefer to make your own, half baby shampoo and half water works fine.

Our favorite trick is to pre-apply no-fog solution to the dry masks an hour or more ahead and let it dry. When you get to the water, just rinse out the mask thoroughly. This seems to last a long time.

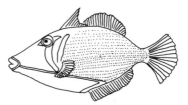

lei triggerfish

Getting Comfortable

After you rinse your mask, try its fit. Adjust the mask strap and snorkel until they're comfortable. Hold the snorkel in your mouth without tightening your jaws. It can be quite loose without falling out. Putting your mask on long before you enter the water can cause it to fog from your exertions

Getting Wet

Now retrieve your fins and walk back in the water, watching the waves carefully. NEVER turn your back on the ocean for long, lest a rogue wave sneak up on you and whack you good.

21

Snorkeling Is Easier than Swimming

Some folks never learn to snorkel because they're not confident as swimmers. This is an unnecessary loss because snorkeling is actually easier than swimming. We have maintained this to friends for years, and noted their doubtful looks. Recently, we came across a program in California that actually uses snorkeling as a tool to help teach swimming!

The Transpersonal Swimming Institute in California specializes in the teaching of adults who are afraid of the water. Local heated pools are used all year. But the warm, salty and buoyant ocean is the best pool of all.

Melon Dash, Director of TSI, takes groups of her students to the Big Island of Hawai'i where they begin by floating comfortably in the warm, salty water. At their own pace, they gradually learn to snorkel and feel comfortable in the water. For people further from California, a video called The Miracle Swimmer is available by mail.

"We have found that people cannot learn what to do with their arms and legs while they are afraid that they might not live."

With a steady air supply and not having to worry about breathing in water accidentally, they can relax and learn the arm and leg movements at ease. Happily, they soon discover there's nothing complicated about it!

In calm conditions and warm water, there need be no age limits and few physical limits for snorkeling.

Transpersonal Swimming Institute   (800) 723-7946
P.O. Box 6543   (510) 526-6000
Albany, CA 94706-0543   fax (510) 526-6091

Transwim@aol.com   www.conquerfear.com

If the bottom is sandy smooth, wade on out until you're about waist deep. Pull your mask on, making sure you remove any stray hair from under the skirt. Position the snorkel in your mouth and start breathing. You can practice this in a pool or hot tub.

Duck down in the water so you're floating and pull on your fins just like sneakers. Be sure no sand is trapped in the fins. Make a smooth turn to your stomach, pause to float and relax until you're comfortable, and you're off! Flip those fins and you have begun your re-entry into the sea.

As you float, practice steady breathing through the snorkel. Breathe slowly and deeply. People sometimes tense up at first and take short breaths. When this happens, you're only getting stale air from the snorkel rather than lots of fresh air from outside. If you ever feel tired or out of breath, don't take off your mask. Just stop as long as necessary, float, breathe easy and relax.

After you've become quite comfortable breathing this way, check how your mask is doing. Make sure it isn't leaking. Adjust the strap if needed. And keep adjusting until it's just right. Slide your snorkel strap to a comfortable position, with the tube pointing about straight up as you float looking down at about a 30° angle.

Swimming while snorkeling is easy once you've relaxed. No arms are required. What works best is to hold your arms straight back along your sides, keep your legs fairly straight and kick those fins slowly without bending your knees much. Any swimming technique will work, of course, but some are more tiring. Practice using the least amount of energy. Once you learn how to snorkel the easy way, you can use all the power you like touring large areas as if you were a migrating whale. But if you're breaking the surface with your fins, going "splash, plunk, splash", you're wasting energy. Be cool and smooth and quiet like a fish.

Clearing Your Mask

Eventually you will need to practice clearing your mask. The Scuba method: take a deep breath, then tip your head up, but with the mask still under the surface. Press your palm to the top of the mask against your forehead, or hold your fingers on the top of the mask and exhale through your nose. This forces water out the bottom of the mask.

Taking It Easy

Relax and try not to push yourself too hard. Experienced snorkelers may urge you on faster than you're comfortable because they've forgotten how it feels to get started. As your experience builds, you'll find it easy too. It's like learning to drive a car. Remember how even a parking lot seemed like a challenge? It helps to practice your beginning snorkeling in a calm easy place—with a patient teacher. With a little persistence, you'll soon overcome your fears and be ready. Don't feel like you should rush. Play around and have fun!

Knowing Your Limits

Have you heard the old saloon saying: "Don't let your mouth write checks that your body can't cover"?

Let's paraphrase this as "Don't let your ego take you places your body can't get you back from." Consider carefully how well-conditioned your legs are, so you'll have enough reserve to be able to make it back home, and then some in case of an emergency.

Snorkeling Alone

In your enthusiasm for the reef, you may wind up in this situation: your significant other prefers watching sports on ESPN to snorkeling one afternoon, and you're sorely tempted to just head out there alone. Don't do it. Snorkeling, done in buddy teams, is a pretty safe recreation, especially if conditions are favorable. Just as in Scuba diving, having a buddy along reduces the risk of a small problem becoming a big problem or even a fatal problem. We won't spell out all the bad things that could happen; we trust your imagination.

Pacing

When you're having a good time, it's easy to forget and over-extend yourself. That next rocky point beckons, and then a pretty spot beyond that. Pretty soon, you're many miles from home and getting tired. Getting cold and overly tired can contribute to poor judgement in critical situations, making you more vulnerable to injury. Why risk turning your great snorkeling experience into a disaster? Learn your limits, and how to pace yourself.

Our favorite technique: If we plan on a one-hour snorkel, we watch the time and start heading back when we've been in the water 30 minutes. If the currents could run against us on the way back, we allow extra time/energy. We like to start by swimming against the current, making the trip home easy and quick.

Caring for Your Gear

You just had a great snorkeling experience—now you can thank the gear that helped make it possible, by taking good care of it.

Rinse and Dry

If there are beach showers, head right up and rinse off. Salt residue is sticky and corrosive. Rinse salt and sand off your wetsuit, fins, mask and snorkel before the saltwater dries. If you can, dry your gear in the shade. It's amazing how much damage sun can do to the more delicate equipment—especially the mask. When the sun odometer hits 100,000 miles, you can kiss those silicon parts goodbye.

Safety Inspections

Keep an eye on vulnerable parts after a few years (strap, snorkel-holder, buckles). Parts are usually easy to find in Hawai'i, but not in the middle of a snorkeling trip unless you're on a well-equipped boat.

If you use any equipment with purge valves, keep an eye on the delicate little flap valves, and replace them when they deteriorate. Masks and snorkels are useless when the valves give way. Remember that many snorkels now have a purge valve at the bottom.

Clean Your Mask

A mask needs a thorough cleaning between trips as well. Unless your mask instructions advise otherwise, use a regular, non-gel toothpaste to clean the lens inside and out, polishing off accumulated goo. Wash the toothpaste off with warm water, using your finger to clean it well.

Potter's angelfish

Hazards

Life just isn't safe. Snorkeling has a few hazards that you should know and avoid if possible. You already know the dangers of car and air travel, yet you mustered your courage and decided that a trip to Hawai'i was worth the risks. And you took reasonable precautions like buckling your seat belt. Well, if you use your noggin, you're probably safer in the water than while driving to get to the water.

Some people are hesitant to snorkel because they imagine meeting a scary creature in the water. But wouldn't you rather be able to see what's down there when you're swimming? We much prefer to see whatever you might step on, run into or encounter. The realities are seldom scary.

We don't think it makes sense to overemphasize certain lurid dangers (sharks!) and pay no attention to the more likely hazard of sunburn which causes more aggravation to tourists.

Sunburn

This is the worst medical problem you're likely to face—especially if you have the wrong ancestors. Use extra water-resistant sunblock in the water and always wear some kind of cover-up during the day. Some people need to avoid the sun entirely from 10 a.m. to 3 p.m., so that's a good excuse to go early and avoid the crowds. The top (or open) deck of a boat is a serious hazard to the easily-burned because bounced rays from the water will double your exposure. The best protection is covering up. Evidence mounts that sunscreen still allows skin damage even though it stops burning. Thanks to recent global warming, we all get more sun in a given hour than we did ten years ago.

When snorkeling, omit sunscreen on your face or hands, because you'll be sorry later if you get the stuff in your eyes. It can really sting and make it difficult to see well enough to navigate back to shore. To avoid using gallons of sunblock, some snorkelers wear lycra body suits. Others simply wear some old clothing.

Take an old sun hat to leave on the beach with your gear bag, especially if you have to hike midday across a reflective white beach. Take old sunglasses that are not theft-worthy. If you must leave prescription glasses on the beach, use your old ones. Kailua-Kona is a great place to find amazingly cheap sunglasses and flip-flops. For long hours in the sun, look into the better sunglasses that carefully filter all the most damaging rays.

Understanding Waves

Waves are travelling ripples in the water, mostly generated by wind blowing over large expanses of water. Having considerable energy, the waves keep going until something stops them. They may travel many thousands of miles before dissipating that energy. Here is the wellspring of the breaking surf. That beautiful surf can also be the biggest danger facing snorkelers.

Take time to sit on a high point and watch the waves approaching the coast, and you will see patterns emerge. Usually there is an underlying groundswell from one direction, waves that may have originated in distant storms. This is the main source of the rhythmical breaking waves, rising and falling in size in noticeable patterns. Sometimes there will be a smaller secondary groundswell from another direction. Often, there will be a series of small waves, followed by one or more larger waves, and the cycle repeats. Pay attention to the patterns and it will be less likely that you'll get caught by surprise.

Local winds add extra energy in their own directions. In Hawai'i, snorkeling is usually easiest in the mornings, before the daily winds create chop and larger waves. Most excursions head out early to make sure they have smooth sailing and calm snorkeling. Sometimes afternoon excursions are offered at reduced prices to compensate for expected rougher conditions.

Occasionally a set of larger waves or a single large rogue wave comes in with little or no warning. A spot that was protected by an offshore reef suddenly has breaking waves. This change can happen while you're out, and make coming back difficult.

Our single worst moment in many years of snorkeling and diving was at Po'ipu Beach Park in Kaua'i after Hurricane Iniki had scattered boulders throughout the beach. We had no problem snorkeling around the boulders in a light swell, protected by reef further out. Suddenly much larger swell crossed the reef and began breaking over us, sweeping everyone back and forth against the boulders, with some resultant bruises.

Since then we have been extra careful to avoid potentially hazardous situations. We always take time to study the waves before entering and ponder what would happen if they suddenly grew much larger, and what our strategy would be. Sometimes we just head for a calmer beach.

Rip Currents

Hawai'i does not have large barrier reefs to intercept incoming waves. Many of the Hawai'ian beaches are exposed to powerful ocean currents—especially in the winter or during storms.

Waves breaking against a shore push volumes of water up close to the shore. As this piles up, it has to flow back to the ocean, and often flows sideways along the shore until it reaches a convenient, often deeper-bottomed, exit point. There, a fast, narrow river of water flows out at high speed. Rip currents, which can carry swimmers out quickly, are of limited duration by their very nature and usually stop no more than 100 yards out.

Sometimes it's possible to swim sideways, but often it's better to simply ride it out. Don't panic. Although the current might be very strong, it won't take you far or drown you, unless you exhaust yourself by swimming against it. It's very easy to float in salt water until help arrives—assuming you're at a beach where someone can see you. Don't try to swim in through waves where there's any chance of being mashed on lava rocks or coral. Don't swim against the current to the point of exhaustion. When in doubt, float and conserve energy.

Even at the most protected beaches all the water coming in must get out, so when swells are up, there's a current somewhere. Big waves beyond the breakwater may seem harmless, but the more water comes in, the more must get out. This is a good reason to ALWAYS wear fins.

Rip currents should not be confused with offshore currents, such as the infamous "Tahiti Express". There are some major flows of water offshore that can be faster than you can swim, even with fins. Do be alert and careful if you swim out beyond rocky points. Or send us a postcard from Tahiti.

Hypothermia

Open ocean water is always cooler than your body, and it cools you off more rapidly than the air. With normal exertion, your body still cools bit by bit. After awhile (perhaps 30-45 minutes) most of us start feeling chilly. Later, shivering begins. When your temperature drops even further, hypothermia sets in. When your body temperature has dropped enough, your abilities to move and even think become impaired.

We used to think hypothermia was just an interesting concept, until it happened to us after a long snorkel in some unusually cold water. We were shivering, but having a great time, and snorkeled on and on. Fortunately, we noticed the decrease in our co-ordination and headed in while we still could. You'd have laughed to see us stumbling clumsily out of the waves. We headed straight for the nearest jacuzzi, shivering and shaking. As we warmed up, our limbs tingled like fizzy water was going through our veins.

One of the first symptoms of hypothermia is poor judgement. Buddies can watch out for each other better than you can watch out for yourself alone—one example of the benefits of having a partner. Check up on each other often in cold conditions.

As soon as you are aware that you're cold, it's time to plan your way back. When shivering starts, you should get out of the water. Be particularly careful in situations requiring all your judgement and skill to be safe, especially when diving, night snorkeling, dealing with waves, or when anticipating a difficult exit from the water.

In Hawai'i, it's usually easy to warm up rapidly since the air temperature is fairly warm at sea level. Even without hypothermia, it's good to warm up between snorkels. If you came by car, it will probably be nicely solar-heated by the time you return.

Sea Urchins

Probably the most common critter injury is stepping on a spiny sea urchin and walking away with lots of spines under your skin. The purple-black spiny sea urchins with long spines tend to appear in large numbers in some areas and favor shallow water, so watch carefully if you see even one. Full-foot flippers or booties help a lot, but don't guarantee protection. Watch where you put your hands—especially in shallow water.

While many folks recommend seeing a doctor for urchin spine slivers, others prefer to just let the spines fester and pop out weeks later. Remove as much spine as you can. Vinegar (or other acidic liquid) will make it feel better. Soaking in Epsom salts helps and the small spines will dissolve in a few weeks, but see a doctor at any sign of infection.

Barracudas

The great barracuda can grow to two meters, has sharp teeth and strong jaws, and swims like a torpedo. For years Judy has removed earrings before swimming after hearing rumors that they attract barracuda, but we've uncovered absolutely no confirming reports of severed ear-ringed ears.

Barracudas are capable of seriously injuring a swimmer so should be taken seriously. Those teeth are just as sharp as they look. Barracudas appear to have attitude, and apparently sometimes do. Our own preference is to respect their territory and allow them some space. Other varieties of barracuda such as the Heller's appear more innocuous.

Once a five-foot great barracuda swam directly beneath us in the Caribbean and appeared annoyed that we were invading his home territory (or so we thought from the fierce look on his face). A usually calm and steady German surgeon snorkeling with us panicked and headed up the nearest rocks as if she could fly. The rest of us snorkeled by him repeatedly with no problem, but didn't appreciate the look he gave us. We later came to realize that they always look grumpy, but seldom bite, like some folks you may know. Perhaps the bigger danger comes from eating the delicious barracuda meat, sometimes containing ciguatera, which is toxic to humans.

great barracuda

Portuguese Man-of-War

The Portuguese man-of-war floats on top, looking like a sailfin one to four inches in size, with extremely long stinging filaments that are quite painful. Stay out of the water if you see one. Even avoid dead ones on the sand! They're very pretty in lovely shades of purple, but can cause severe pain.

Vinegar or unseasoned meat tenderizer helps ease the sting and helps stop the release of venom from the stinging cells if tentacles are clinging to you. Use wet sand as a last resort. If you feel ill, see a doctor right away. If jellyfish are present, locals will know which ones are harmful. Jellyfish have seldom been a problem for us in Hawai'i. In all our years in the water in Hawai'i, we've only been stung by a Portuguese man-of-war once—we didn't see the jelly-fish itself, but sure noticed the long red welt!

Rays

Sting rays prefer to avoid you, but hang out on the bottom where they're easy to step on. They prefer resting in calm water that is slightly warmer than the surrounding area — just the areas favored by people for swimming. Step on them and they may sting you, so the injury is usually to the foot or ankle. They can inflict a serious or painful sting to people—especially children. It's best to get immediate first aid and follow up with medical assistance.

In this case snorkelers have an advantage over swimmers because snorkelers can see sting rays and easily avoid them. In Maui we've seen them swim between children's legs in shallow water at Kapalua Bay and were amazed to see how adept the rays were at avoiding people.

Manta rays don't sting, but they're much larger. They are often six to eight feet across weighing several hundred pounds. They maneuver beautifully, so don't pose any danger. With a little luck, you'll be able to see one of these beautiful creatures.

manta ray

31

Poisonous Fish

Lionfish (also called turkeyfish) and scorpionfish have spines which are very poisonous. Don't step on or touch them! Their poison can cause serious pain and infection or allergic reaction, so definitely see a doctor if you have a close, personal encounter with one. Fins or booties can help protect your tender feet.

Scorpionfish can blend in so well along the bottom in shallow water that they're easy to miss. Turkeyfish, though, are colorful and easy to spot. Since these fish are not abundant in Hawai'i, they are treasured sightings. You are not likely to encounter one in casual snorkeling.

Hawai'ian turkeyfish

Eels

Eels are rarely aggressive and often tamed by divers. Most do possess a formidable array of teeth, which should be avoided. An eel bite can definitely cause serious bleeding requiring prompt medical attention. Another good reason not to snorkel alone!

Eels are fascinating and easy to find in Hawai'i. Count on eels to make every effort to avoid you, so there's no need to panic at the sight of one—even if it's swimming freely. Eels aren't interested in humans as food, but they do want to protect themselves and can usually do so with ease by slipping away into the nearest hole. Do we need to tell you to keep your hands out of crevices in the coral?

leopard moray eel

Cone Shells

The snails inside these pretty black and brown-decorated shells can fire a poisonous dart. The venom can cause a serious reaction or even death—especially to allergic persons. If in doubt, head for a doctor. If you never pick up underwater shells, you won't have any problem.

cone shell

Drowning

Not likely to happen to you, but we want to help you become so alert and prepared that you have a safe vacation.

We looked up the statistics for the past 30 years, and they are both comforting and cautionary. Only a few people drown each year on the Big Island. A much lower number than fatalities from auto wrecks, industrial accidents, or probably even accidents at home.

A couple things stand out about who are the victims. Three out of four victims are visitors. Not too surprising, since you assume locals are more aware of the hazards. But nine out of ten are males, mostly 20 to 50 years old! You'd think this would be a low-risk group.

What leads these males to get into a dangerous situation? Well, some guys just can't help overrating their athletic prowess, and underestimating the power of the ocean.

Some locations seem distinctly more hazardous. Popular Hapuna Beach with its big waves in the winter is the Big Island's most hazardous site. Big, calm bays like Kealakekua offer very safe snorkeling. Secluded beaches can be dangerous since no help is available if you get in trouble.

It's easy to swim and snorkel in Big Island waters safely. Improve your odds by picking only protected beaches and bays when the surf is pounding. Watch for swells and currents when storms arrive. Don't overestimate your stamina. Perhaps you might follow our personal rule: always wear fins when swimming in the open ocean in Hawai'i. And, always snorkel with a buddy.

Sharks

Sharks are seldom a problem for snorkelers. In Hawai'i the modest number of verified shark attacks have mostly occurred off O'ahu with tiger sharks the major perpetrator, and surfers the major targets. Sharks often hunt in very murky river runoff, but most snorkelers avoid these conditions anyway.

We have read that, according to statistics, you're more likely to be killed by a pig than a shark. We take great comfort in that, as I'm sure you do, too; though we've quit eating bacon just in case.

Some people will suggest you can pet, feed or even tease certain types of shark. We personally would give sharks a bit of respect and leave them entirely in peace. Most sharks are well-fed on fish and not all that interested in well-oiled tourists, but it's hard to tell by looking at a shark whether it has had a bad day.

Sharks usually feed late in the day or at night, causing some people to prefer to enjoy the water more in the morning or midday. If you're in an area frequented by sharks, this might be good to keep in mind. We must admit that we snorkel at any hour, and occasionally night snorkel. The few sharks we have seen have all been midday.

In Hawai'i, with luck, you might possibly see sandbar, black-tip, white-tip or even hammerhead sharks—more often in deep water sites like the middle of Kealakekua Bay. If you do, stay calm, and appreciate your opportunity to glimpse these sleek creatures.

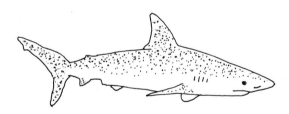

reef shark

I Like to Watch

"For some reason, the barracuda don't seem scary, any more than the ray does. For some reason, none of this seems scary. Even the idea of maybe encountering a smallish s___k doesn't seem altogether bad.

It's beginning to dawn on me that all the fish and eels and crabs and shrimps and plankton who live and work down here are just too busy to be thinking about me.

I'm a traveller from another dimension, not really a part of their already event-filled world, not programmed one way or another—food or yikes—into their instinct circuits. They have important matters to attend to, and they don't care whether I watch or not. And so I watch."

—Dave Barry

Snorkeling Sites

Where are those big beautiful fish?

The Big Island is as large as all the other major Hawai'ian islands together, and offers an excellent variety of good snorkeling sites. We've started at the end of the road going north from Kailua-Kona, then continue counter-clockwise around the island. Most of the best and more reliable sites are along the more protected western coast—especially in South Kohala, North Kona and South Kona.

As we begin our description of individual sites, we start in the district of North Kohala, where winter often brings big waves. These sites can be very dangerous when rough, but calm as bathwater on a good day. When swells roll in, they are best left to experienced snorkelers, who understand the challenges and can safely swim in isolated locations.

The South Kohala district has become very popular with tourists because of its nearly year-round sun. Here you find large hotels located on lovely wide bays, as well as equally beautiful sites that require some hiking. Most of this section of coast is lava with an oasis here and there near the coast where fresh water often provides pools. Many of these beautiful bays are at least partially protected, and can be fairly calm—especially when the swells don't hit directly. Wind can pick up around noon, so these sites are typically calmest in the early morning.

The popular Mauna Kea and Mauna Lani resorts offer beautiful sites along the edges of big bays. Excellent and safe snorkeling awaits. Puako, Wai'alea, and Hapuna also offer excellent snorkeling, but only when waves aren't too high.

North Kona includes the airport, where most of you will arrive. While the coast here is mostly moonscape lava, there are some excellent small sites with palm trees, sand and great snorkeling. Few of the hotels are located here. Most of the sites require a hike, but often only a short, easy one. Tiny coves on either side of Honokohau Harbor can be reached by all, while Makalawena Bay is a long, hot hike over a rough lava path, but offers a serene bay surrounded by sand dunes.

Kailua-Kona is the largest city on this side of the island and has numerous hotels and condos—something for everyone at every price. Attractions include easy Kahalu'u Beach to night snorkeling with the mantas at Keauhou, with many small sandy beaches scattered all along Ali'i Drive.

South Kona offers an excellent variety of snorkeling sites—from top snorkeling near the Captain Cook monument, to Place of Refuge with its extraordinary Two Step snorkeling site. Kealakeakua Bay near the monument requires boat, kayak, horseback or difficult on-foot access. Two Step, near Place of Refuge, simply requires good directions because it's easy to miss the road completely.

The Ka'u district is located in the far south and tends to get abundant wind from the south. While not loaded with snorkeling sites, it's still worth the drive when south swells are low. Our favorite site here is Green Sand Beach (Mahana Bay), but it's only for those who are willing to hike three miles each way over bare terrain. It's essential to check conditions first if you plan to snorkel anywhere along south-facing beaches.

The Puna district is the "bump" of the Big Island that sticks out to the east. Just beyond the volcanoes, there are some nice sites here, although they can be rough when southern swells arrive in the summer. An exception is the unusual Wai'opae Tidepools, where waves are seldom a problem.

South Hilo has a long row of easily-reached beaches, but many are not suitable for snorkeling. Our favorite of these is the inner area of Richardson Beach.

North Hilo and Hamakua districts face the northeast, so catch the prevailing northeastern swells. Therefore, they are nearly always too rough for snorkeling or swimming. Access is also blocked by cliffs. We haven't included any sites in this area, but the views are beautiful enough to be worth the long trip.

Weather patterns bring storms to Hawai'i from different directions. In winter, they're often from the north, while summer brings southern storms. Plan your location accordingly or, at the least, prepare to drive a bit if conditions aren't good where you're staying. There's nearly always a calm beach with easy snorkeling and swimming. One of the calmest on the Big Island is Kahalu'u Beach. It might get too rough a couple of days each year, but is a good bet when conditions are too rough elsewhere.

We've snorkeled for many years around all the major Hawai'ian islands. For snorkeling, the Big Island has become our sentimental favorite. For brief notes on our favorites spots, check Snorkeling Sites at a Glance (page 40). For detailed information and maps, locate the sites on our Site Map (page 38). All listings begin in the north and proceed counter-clockwise around the island. Area maps are designed to help you locate a site, while site maps give you more specific details.

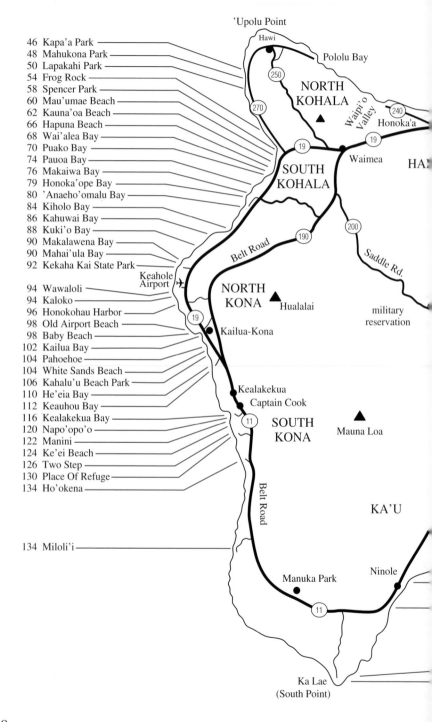

'Upolu Point
Hawi
Pololu Bay
250
NORTH
KOHALA
270
Waipi'o Valley
240
Honoka'a
19
19
Waimea
SOUTH
KOHALA
HA:
200
190
Belt Road
Saddle Rd.
Keahole
Airport
NORTH
KONA
Hualalai
military
reservation
19
Kailua-Kona
Kealakekua
Captain Cook
11
SOUTH
KONA
Mauna Loa
KA'U
Belt Road
Ninole
Manuka Park
11
Ka Lae
(South Point)

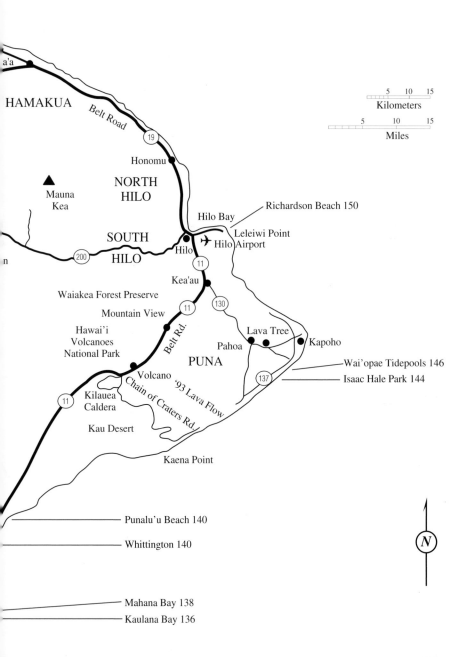

a'a

HAMAKUA

Belt Road

19

Honomu

▲ Mauna Kea

NORTH HILO

Hilo Bay

Richardson Beach 150

Leleiwi Point
Hilo Airport

SOUTH HILO

200

Hilo

11

Kea'au

Waiakea Forest Preserve

Mountain View

11

130

Hawai'i Volcanoes National Park

Lava Tree

Belt Rd.

Pahoa

Kapoho

PUNA

Wai'opae Tidepools 146

Volcano

137

Isaac Hale Park 144

11

Kilauea Caldera

Chain of Craters Rd.

'93 Lava Flow

Kau Desert

Kaena Point

Punalu'u Beach 140

Whittington 140

N

Mahana Bay 138

Kaulana Bay 136

Kilometers

5   10   15

Miles

5   10   15

Sites at a Glance

	SNORKELING	ENTRY	SANDY BEACH	RESTROOM	SHOWERS	PICNIC AREA	SCENIC	SHADE
Kapa'a Park	C	1-3	•	•		•		•
Mahukona Park	A	1-3		•	•	•		•
Lapakahi Park	A	1-3		•			•	
Frog Rock	A	1-3					•	
Spencer Park	C	1-2	•	•	•	•	•	•
Mau'umae Beach	A	1	•				•	•
Kauna'oa (Mauna Kea)	A	1	•	•	•	•	•	•
Hapuna Beach	A	1-3	•	•	•	•	•	•
Wai'alea Bay (69)	A	1-2	•				•	•
Puako Bay—N	A	1					•	
Puako Bay—S	A	1-3				•	•	•
Pauoa Bay (Orchid)	C	1	•	•	•	•	•	•
Makaiwa (Mauna Lani)	A	1	•	•	•		•	•
Honoka'ope Beach	B	1-2	•	•		•	•	•
'Anaeho'omalu—N	A	1	•	•	•	•	•	•
'Anaeho'omalu—S	C	1	•	•	•	•	•	•
Kiholo Bay	A	1	•			•	•	•
Kahuwai (Kona Village)	A	1	•	•	•		•	•
Kuki'o (Four Seasons)			•	•	•		•	•
Makalawena Beach	B	1	•	•		•	•	•
Mahai'ula Beach	B	1	•	•		•	•	•
Kekaha Kai Park	B	1-3	•	•		•	•	•
Wawaloli Park				•	•	•	•	•
Honokohau Harbor—N	C	1	•	•	•	•	•	•
Honokohau Harbor—S	B	1	•	•	•	•	•	•
Old Kona Airport	A	2	•	•	•	•	•	•
Baby Beach			•				•	•
Kamakahonu Beach	B	1	•				•	•

PAGE	MAP PAGE	NOTES
46	45	rather rundown, need high tide for clearance, often rough
48	49	ladder entry from parking, simple shower, remains of ship
50	51	historic, protected reef, secluded, dangerous when rough
54	55	extensive, secluded & varied reef, requires short hike
58	57	big, family park, camping, some snorkeling, all facilities
60	61	secluded, gorgeous bay, need pass & must hike
62	63	beautiful, come early for pass, excellent in every way
66	67	popular, big park, often rough in winter & afternoons
68	69	short hike, secluded, sandy beach, delightful when calm
70	71	swim out long boat channel to far edge of excellent reef
72	71	broad, shallow reef, swim around rather than over reef
74	75	facilities at park, hike to snorkeling in front of the Orchid
76	77	3/4-mile hike from parking & facilities, large reef, calm
79	77	"black" sand, small, easy public access, near Makaiwa
80	81	long swim to outer part of reef for best visibility
80	81	popular, all water sports, not clear or great, long beach
84	85	over 1-mile hike, shallow & lovely bay, small fish, turtles
86	87	best in morning, requires hike from public parking
88	87	wading pools in front, walk along sand to Kahuwai
90	91	lovely, secluded, requires rough lava hike from Kekaha Kai
90	91	lovely, fairly secluded, easy hike from Kekaha Kai
92	91	often rougher than nearby beaches, wide area to explore
94	83	deep water here & very rough, best for picnic
96	97	high tide essential, small & shallow bay
96	97	tiny, protected cove, nice beach, snorkel beyond point
98	99	high tide best for entry, good snorkeling beyond point
98	99	lovely, secluded small cove for wading, shallow & safe
102	103	central location, but still good snorkeling around point

Sites at a Glance

	SNORKELING	ENTRY	SANDY BEACH	RESTROOM	SHOWERS	PICNIC AREA	SCENIC	SHADE
Kailua-Kona Pier	B	1	•				•	•
Pahoehoe Park	B	1-3	•			•	•	•
La'aloa (White Sands)	B	1-3	•	•	•	•	•	•
Kahalu'u Beach	A	1	•	•	•	•	•	•
He'eia Bay	B	1-3						•
Keauhou Bay	B	1		•	•	•	•	
Captain Cook Monument	A	1					•	•
Kealakekua Park	B	1-3	•			•	•	•
Napo'opo'o Pier	B	1				•	•	•
Manini Beach	B	1-2				•	•	•
Ke'ei Beach	B	1-3	•			•	•	•
Honaunau (Two Step)	A+	1-2	•			•	•	•
Place of Refuge—North	A	1-2	•	•		•	•	•
Place of Refuge—South	A	1-3	•			•	•	•
Ho'okena Beach	B	2	•	•	•	•	•	•
Miloli'i Beach	B	2	•			•	•	•
Kaulana (South Point)	B	1	•				•	•
Mahana (Green Sands)	B	1-3	•				•	
Whittington Park	B	1-3	•	•	•	•	•	•
Punalu'u Beach	C	2-3	•	•	•	•	•	•
Isaac Hale Park	B	1	•	•	•	•	•	•
Wai'opae Tidepools	A	1					•	
Richardson Park	A	1-2	•	•	•	•	•	

A Excellent	1 Easy
B Good	2 Moderate
C Fair	3 Difficult

PAGE	MAP PAGE	NOTES
102	103	handy, good snorkeling to right, watch for boats
104	101	lava shoreline, snorkel only when unusually calm
104	101	good when calm, often need to go south to Kahalu'u
106	107	popular, but crowded, large fish, turtles, coral damage
110	111	small, protected bay, somewhat shallow, no crowds
112	113	good with few boats, best toward point so requires swim
116	117	excellent, with spectacular location, often spinner dolphins
120	121	rocky beach, but good snorkeling to left along lava
120	121	easy entry from old pier when fairly calm, wide area
122	121	rocky beach, can access Kealakekua Bay when tide up
124	125	large area to explore only when calm, secluded, rough road
126	127	the best, entry from lava, free parking goes early, don't miss!
130	131	canoe entrance to bay, nothing can be left on beach
132	131	entry from lava when calm, usually not for beginners
134	115	wide & shallow reef, poor facilities, need calm water
134	4	Hawai'ian Lands area, tourists better off coming by boat
136	137	bare area, but good snorkeling when south swell low
138	139	only when calm, 3-mile hike, no facilities, but beautiful
140	4	several beaches & tidepools, but need low south swells
140	4	black sand beach, rocky entry, often dangerous
144	147	enter near pier when calm, warm pools nearby
146	147	unique, uncrowded, treat with care, no fins needed
150	149	rocky, but broad protected area, likely to rain, cooler

43

North Kohala area

Few tourists make it to the farthest points in North Kohala, so it remains a charming, relatively noncommercial corner of the island. Towns are tiny, the ocean is often rougher here, and the landscape diverse. No big hotels or condos and little traffic, just a lovely drive to the end of Highway 270 at the beautiful Pololu Valley Lookout. You can return by way of Highway 250 through the upcountry of the Kohala Mountains and the green, forested town of Waimea. Stop in the little town of Hawi for lunch and visit beautiful Keokea Beach Park while you're up this way.

If you want to count on being able to enjoy the water, check surf conditions before heading to North Kohala on a long day trip. These northern sites are often too rough for safe water sports— especially in the winter.

We've listed snorkeling sites starting at the far north of the island, where swells are often high. Conditions become more favorable as we continue counter-clockwise around the Big Island of Hawai'i, with the most reliable snorkeling found in the areas of South Kohala, North Kona and South Kona.

On a calm day, the west coast of North Kohala has several excellent sites. All are quite secluded, so you might be the only people in the water. For this reason, we urge extra caution—especially if you're new to the island or new to snorkeling. Each site is unique, so water conditions can vary considerably on a given day.

One of our favorite sites in Hawai'i is Frog Rock, located along this coast. Large swells can make the entry dangerous, but flat water makes it easy enough for a beginner. The hike is short and the location beautiful, so be sure to check it out when you're up this way.

Lapakahi Park, further north, is also worth the drive—for the snorkel as well as a visit to the historical park.

Mahukona Bay, although near Lapakahi, offers a different snorkeling experience. Here you enter from a ladder and snorkel within an old harbor area. Look for pieces of an old wreck on the ocean floor.

When conditions are favorable, try some of these northern sites, but always watch awhile to assess the swells before you snorkel. Early risers almost always get the calmest water. There is usually plenty of light for snorkeling by 8 a.m., and the water is often flat, calm and beautiful then. By 10-11 a.m., the wind-driven swell may come up, and it's a whole different snorkeling world.

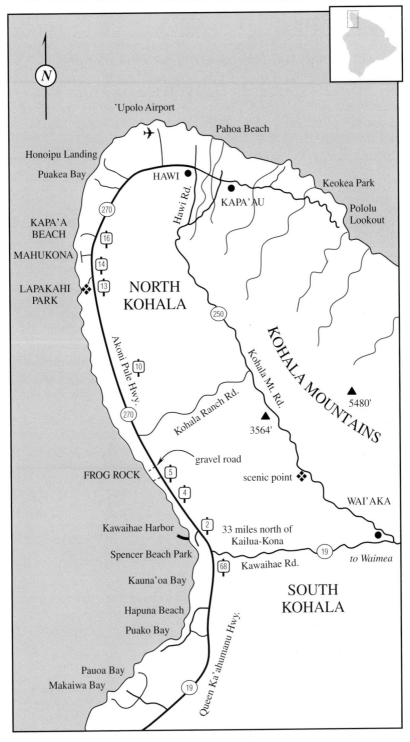

N

'Upolo Airport

Pahoa Beach

Honoipu Landing

Puakea Bay

HAWI

Hawi Rd.

Keokea Park

KAPA'AU

Pololu
Lookout

KAPA'A
BEACH

270

16

MAHUKONA

14

250

LAPAKAHI
PARK

13

NORTH
KOHALA

KOHALA MOUNTAINS

Akoni Pule Hwy.

10

Kohala Mt. Rd.

5480'

270

Kohala Ranch Rd.

3564'

gravel road

FROG ROCK

5

scenic point

WAI'AKA

4

Kawaihae Harbor

2

33 miles north of
Kailua-Kona

Spencer Beach Park

68

19

to Waimea

Kauna'oa Bay

Kawaihae Rd.

SOUTH
KOHALA

Hapuna Beach

Puako Bay

Queen Ka'ahumanu Hwy.

Pauoa Bay

Makaiwa Bay

19

Kapa'a Park

Located near the Big Island's far north, just a short hop from Highway 270, Kapa'a Park is the first snorkeling site on our list. We start here at the north and proceed with the sites counter-clockwise. North Kohala usually has rougher water and offers much less in the way of facilities than you will find along the South Kohala coast. On a calm day, the snorkeling can be surprisingly easy.

Any sites further north than Kapa'a Park are unlikely to offer safe snorkeling in most weather. Kapa'a itself is often uncomfortably rough, and should be skipped if questionable.

Kapa'a Park includes a small, somewhat protected bay with a rocky black and white "beach." Facilities include a small parking lot, picnic tables and portapotties, but no drinking water. It could stand some renovation. Snorkeling is good, but best if you snorkel to the left and beyond the point—water conditions permitting.

Summer is the best time to find easy swimming here because winter swells can make this part of the North Kohala coast hazardous. Mornings are nearly always calmer, with wind picking up by noon. When swells are low, you can snorkel south along the cliff as far as you like, exploring small coves along the way. You will often see an octopus among the rocks if you look very closely.

GETTING THERE   Head north on Highway 19, then stay left on Highway 270 rather than taking the right to Waimea. Follow the signs to Mahukona. Kapa'a is located at mile marker 16 just north of Mahukona (see map, page 45). Turn makai (toward the ocean) and drive .7 of a mile to the end of the road. You can't miss the little park and are likely to have it entirely to yourselves.

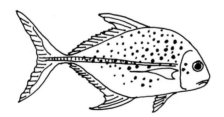

bluefin trevally jack

Snuba

Snuba® was developed as a simpler alternative to Scuba for shallow dives in resort conditions. Because Snuba divers are strictly limited in depth and conditions, and are always accompanied by an guide, the orientation takes just 15-30 minutes.

Two people share a small inflatable raft, which holds a Scuba air tank. A twenty-foot hose leads from the tank to a light harness on each diver. A comfortable weight belt completes your outfit. Very light and tropical!

Once in the water, your guide teaches you to breathe through your regulator (which has a mouthpiece just like your snorkel) on the surface until you're completely comfortable. You're then free to swim around as you like, remembering to clear your ears as needed-limited by the hose to twenty feet deep, of course.

The raft will automatically follow you as you tour the reef. It's that easy! You have to be at least eight years old, and have normal good health. Kids do amazingly well, and senior citizens can also enjoy Snuba. There's even a new program called Snuba Doo for 4 to 7-year old children. They wear a floatation vest, and breathe through a regulator as they float on the surface while their parents Snuba below.

We are certified Scuba divers, yet we actually enjoy Snuba more. Less gear equals more fun. Snuba is a lot like snorkeling, with the added freedom to move on down close to fish and coral. We often surface dive to check out what fish is hiding under a coral head. Snuba is like surface diving without having to come up for air!

Snuba provides a fun and safe experience if you pay attention and do it as directed. Their safety record is superb.

Warning: do pay attention to the instructions because even at these shallow depths, you must know the proper way to surface. You must remember to never hold your breath as you ascend or you could force a bubble of air into your blood. Breathing out continually while surfacing is not intuitive, but is absolutely necessary when you're breathing compressed air. This is especially important to remember if you're used to surface diving where you always hold your breath. Dive safely!

Mahukona Park

Less than a mile north of Lapakahi, you'll find this small park with a boat launch, ample parking, a basic shower, restrooms, picnic tables, but no beach and no drinking water. Snorkeling and swimming are possible from a ladder down into about five feet of water, sloping out to about twenty feet deep.

You'll find a simple shower at the right side of the parking lot. The ladder is straight in front (left of the shower). Don't attempt to swim or snorkel here when heavy swells arrive in the winter. We snorkeled in water calm enough for a 3-year-old, but just days later a young man died after being swept into the lava rocks in heavy swells. These swells can really sweep past the steps as they funnel into the shallow water of the inner area.

If you're planning to snorkel anywhere in North Kohala, check the wave reports before you drive this far. Mahukona is not as pristine as nearby Lapakahi, but access is much easier. The park is small and uncrowded, so entry is just steps from your car. Mahukona is primarily a boulder habitat, but has a fair amount of coral patches, with plenty of big fish. Snorkeling to either the north or south will take you over some relics from the steamship "Kaua'i" that sank here in 1913. Look for a huge anchor to the left and propeller to the right—both are nearby. We recently encountered an unusually bold octopus in the shallower area near the ladder. It displayed nearly every color and texture in its repertoire, and didn't attempt to hide. Larger fish frequent this site, so watch for numerous bigeye emperor fish.

If you snorkel at Lapakahi, nearby Mahukona Park provides a convenient spot to shower and picnic. Consider a day trip that takes you past Hawi, to the end of Highway 270 to see the Pololu Valley, then back through upcountry Wailea. You may also enjoy a stop at scenic Keokea State Park, but the north-facing coast is usually far too rough for good snorkeling. Keokea does have all facilities and a shallow, sheltered area to the right that provides a safe spot for a dip.

GETTING THERE   Head north on Highway 19, then continue to the left on Highway 270 rather than right to Waimea (see area map, page 45). Watch for Lapakahi on your left, then go another .9 of a mile to the Mahukona sign between mile markers 14 and 16, at mile 14.9. Turn toward the ocean. After .4 of a mile, you'll come to a T at the Hawai'i Railroad building (from an old sugarcane railway ending here). The parking lot and boat launch are on the right, while the rest of the park with no water access is to the left. A simple shower can be found on the far right side of the boat launch, while the ladder is directly in front (see map, page 49). Ignore the yellow wasps coming to drink water, and they'll ignore you—they seem quite passive.

48

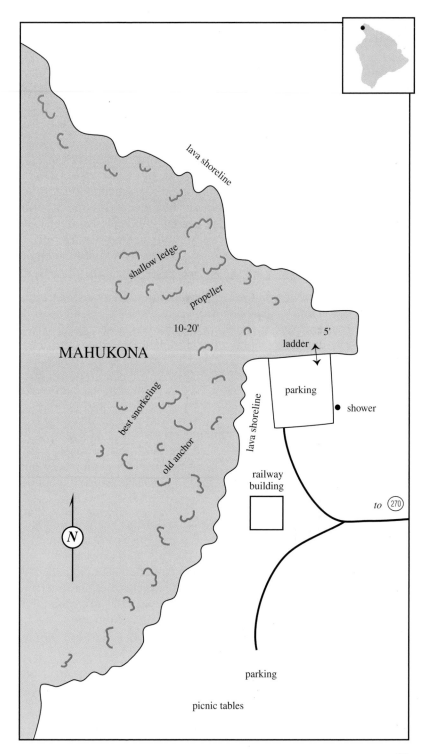

lava shoreline

shallow ledge

propeller

10-20'

5'

ladder

MAHUKONA

parking

shower

best snorkeling

lava shoreline

old anchor

railway
building

to 270

N

parking

picnic tables

49

Lapakahi Park

Lapakahi Marine Life Conservation and State Historical Park has a serene, somewhat austere beauty. Off the beaten track in North Kohala, it can seem abandoned in the winter. Lapakahi has no running water or showers and little shade on the trail, but there is a cooler of drinking water available.

When you park, stop by the office to check in with the park rangers. They want to make sure everyone treats the park with respect. The rules include no towels or clothing left on the beach and no snorkeling to the left where there are important burial sites. It's OK to leave shoes, hats and glasses, since all are needed to hike down to the beach. And, please, no sunscreen in the water and no fish feeding. These are getting to be more common requests in areas that attempt to protect the natural diversity.

A 300-yard hike takes you directly down to the water—a worthwhile hike even if you don't swim. The trail is on the side of moderate hill. While the trail isn't well marked, it's easy to see the beach. As you near the shore and intersect the main trail parallel to the shore, jog left and enter at the small pebble "beach." Snorkel to the right wherever it appears calmest, but only if conditions are calm. The water to your left is off-limits to the public out of respect for ancient Hawai'ian grave sites.

Lapakahi has good snorkeling, although no showers and a fair access hike with no shade. Entry is across rocks, so don't try if there's any problem with swell. It can be very tricky getting back out if big waves pick up. Early mornings are better here, since the wind usually picks up late morning.

Good swimming skills and fins are essential. Don't venture too far from shore since the currents can be strong. This is a place where you need to sit and watch for awhile. Also, ask park rangers for advice, but keep in mind they may be much better swimmers than you are. Wave size often varies in noticeable cycles, but may also change suddenly (see Understanding Waves, page 27). We snorkeled here one morning when the water was completely calm and thoroughly enjoyed the snorkeling as well as the atmosphere. For the entire snorkel, we were the only visitors to the park.

Marine life is protected and the fish seem to understand, so they are unusually bold. We have seen huge schools of yellow tangs, an octopus, little juvenile yellow coris, and most of the usual reef fish. The coral is quite healthy, but does get plenty of pounding in the winter.

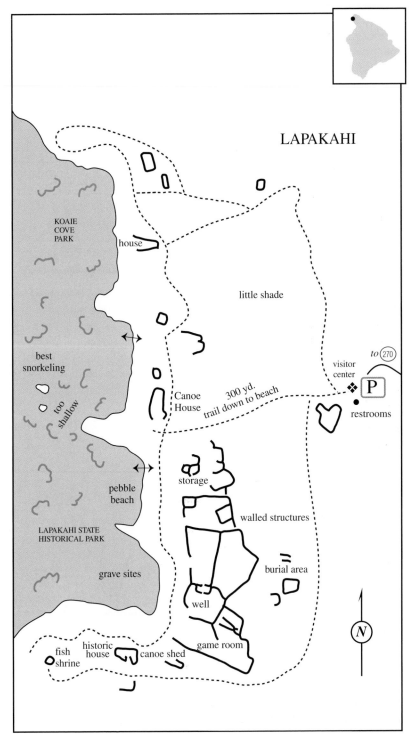

LAPAKAHI

KOAIE
COVE
PARK

house

little shade

best
snorkeling

too
shallow

visitor
center

to 270

P

Canoe
House

300 yd.
trail down to beach

restrooms

pebble
beach

storage

walled structures

LAPAKAHI STATE
HISTORICAL PARK

burial area

grave sites

well

N

fish
shrine

historic
house

canoe shed

game room

Lapakahi is the site of a 13th century fishing village called Koai'a, abandoned in the 1800s when water was diverted for use at the sugar plantations. Stone foundations are all around you and it's now a hot, dry, but very beautiful site. It's hard to compare lovely beaches, but this is definitely a dramatic one. Sit and imagine what it might have been like to live and work in this village when there was more rainfall, and before water was diverted for the sugar cane plantations. When swells are too high, consider trying Mahukona instead, but do visit Lapakahi Park at least once.

GETTING THERE Go north on Highway 19 (see map, page 45), past mile marker 68, and then turn left on Highway 270 near the harbor. You're at mile marker 2 on this road. Watch immediately for a Y (at a gas station) and continue on 270 (the right of the Y) heading north toward Mahukona. Follow 270 (Akuni Pule Highway) north to the Lapakahi sign on the left. It's between mile markers 13 and 14. Notice that they lock the gate at 4 p.m. and the sign suggests that if locked in, you may have to hike a minimum of 7 1/2 miles north to the nearest phone! The total distance from the Kailua-Kona Junction to the Lapakahi turnoff is 46.6 miles. See map, page 51.

The park is usually open from 8 till 4, however, it's best to call ahead if you plan to arrive on a holiday, when it might be closed. We've heard reports of snorkelers being turned away by the one and only park employee, so be prepared to accept an alternative (such as Mahukona) if this happens to you. We've even heard of people being told they couldn't sit. When a park is this remote and has only one person to interpret the rules, you might be stuck. We've never had any problem ourselves and recommend a most respectful attitude to avoid problems.

Petroglyphs

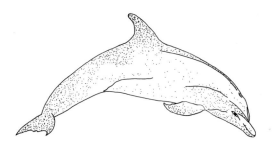

bottlenose dolphin

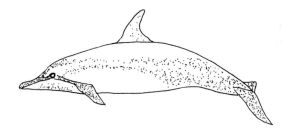

spinner dolphin

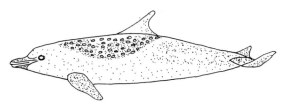

spotted dolphin

Frog Rock

For a delightful and secluded snorkel, Frog Rock, north of Kawaihae Harbor, can be reached from a short dirt road off Highway 270. The water here is clear and the reef area enormous, so you'll want to stay and explore. Since there is no sand, only a boulder beach, access is easy only when seas are very calm. When swells roll in (especially in the winter), Frog Rock can be downright dangerous. When off by yourselves, always snorkel in the morning before wind and swells increase by noon. Also, leave something bright on shore to help guide you back to the entry point.

Follow our directions to this site, then snorkel along the coast in either direction, exploring the small coves full of interesting fish. This is a great place to watch for an octopus.

The peninsulas of reef extend far out to sea, so you can also follow them to see different creatures in the deeper water. The tops of some sections of reef come within about five feet of the surface, sloping down to about 30-50' deep. You may see divers out a ways, but are unlikely to see any snorkelers for miles.

This is one of our favorites for a long snorkel. Check out the arches, tunnels, tiny coves, and huge coral heads. Frog Rock has some of the most beautiful coral in Hawai'i. We once saw four octopuses here close together on the coral.

Such a secluded site is usually for advanced snorkelers only, but beginners who don't mind deep water can enjoy Frog Rock on a very calm day. There are no facilities here, but Kawaihae Harbor has restrooms toward the center and a simple shower at the far north. Spencer Park, south of the harbor, also has full facilities.

GETTING THERE   Head north on Highway 19 (see area map, page 45) and take the Y to the left as it becomes Highway 270 (rather than right to Waimea). Following the signs toward Mahukona, watch for mile marker 5 to the north of Kawaihae Harbor. At .6 of a mile north of marker 5, you'll see a small public access parking lot and trail, which you don't want to waste time on, because it only leads to a cliff. Instead, continue on Highway 270 to .9 of a mile past marker 5.

Here you'll find a gravel road toward the ocean (see site map, page 55). Check it out & either drive the .15 of a mile down to parking or simply park near the highway and walk down the road. Avoid driving the last 50 yards since this stretch is much rougher. As you walk straight toward the water, you'll end up at a "lookout" spot where you can see the 30-yard path down to a storm beach on your right (north). Rather than sand, this beach is lined with chunks of lava. Enter the water from the closest rocks assuming the sea is calm. Please don't take chances here if you have any doubt about the swells.

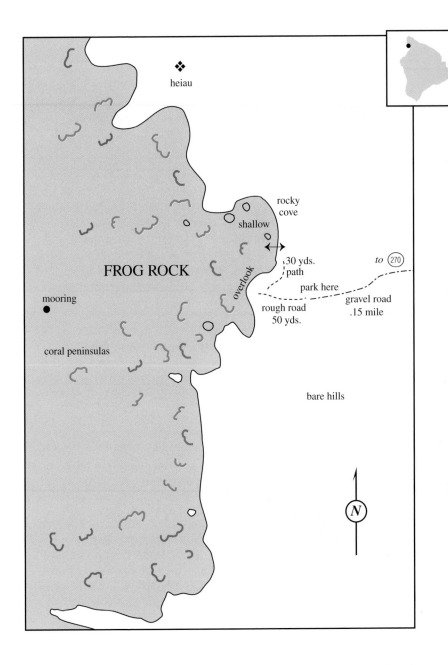

heiau

rocky cove

shallow

FROG ROCK

overlook

30 yds. path

to (270)

park here

mooring

rough road 50 yds.

gravel road .15 mile

coral peninsulas

bare hills

N

They must be low enough to make for a safe exit because there is no alternative exit and no one to rescue you. Water in this tiny cove is about 2-4' deep, so you will want to head out for more comfortable snorkeling.

The hill to the north of this site has a dramatic heiau that can be seen from land or sea, which will confirm that you've found the right spot.

South Kohala area

In recent years, several large resorts have been built in the popular South Kohala area. They promote themselves as "total destination" resorts, and each has its own particular character. Some feel comfortably Hawai'ian; others seem more like theme parks just plopped down complete in a tropical setting. Construction continues, so you'll need to check our web site for updates on the latest resorts.

While many tourists focus on sunning, eating, water slides and golf, there are plenty of excellent reefs along this coast. There's an abundance of sun, little rain, and water conditions that are typically excellent in the morning. Swells and wind tend to pick up around noon and can be impressive, so get yourself out early if in doubt. Many of the beaches front hotels, which provide very limited parking for the public, so the available public parking goes fast. Guard stations are found here and you'll need to know the magic words that work with each.

South Kohala is an excellent snorkeling destination, perhaps even better for snorkeling than for swimming. The Mauna Kea beaches are terrific for both. The Mauna Lani Terrace fronts Makaiwa Bay, where you'll find one of the Big Island's biggest reefs, part of the long reef extending on past Puako.

While the winter will sometimes bring large swells, many of these South Kohala beaches are excellent a good part of the year. Parking is usually the biggest challenge, unless you are staying in the resorts. Some beaches have two public parking areas, so select the one closest to the best snorkeling area.

On occasion, a fierce trade wind blows for days across the low center of the island straight for South Kohala. When this happens, you'll find better conditions either north or south. Kona can be virtually windless while tourists in South Kohala stay indoors to avoid the sand. In very hot weather (especially September), you will appreciate the trade winds. When it's hot and muggy in Kailua-Kona, consider driving up to South Kohala.

Kauna'oa Beach at the Mauna Kea Resort and 'Anaeho'omalu Bay in front of the Outrigger are two of the more popular snorkeling sites in South Kohala. If you're looking for more seclusion, Wai'alea (with its shady beach fringe) and Puako (with a four-mile long reef) also have excellent snorkeling. Hapuna Park and Makaiwa Bay (near the Mauna Lani) are both beautiful with large reefs. South Kohala has enough variety to keep you snorkeling for a long, long time.

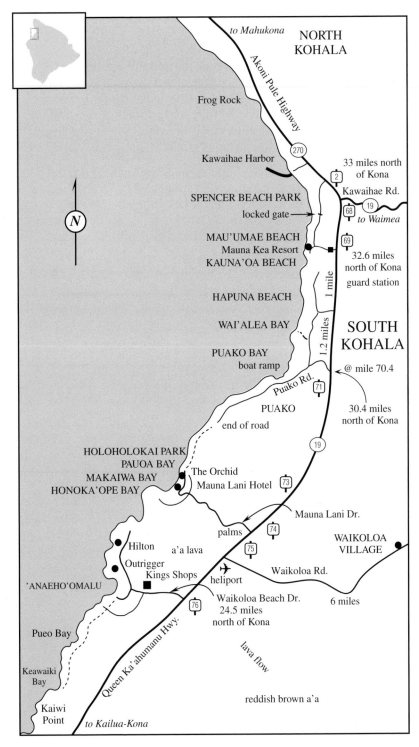

to Mahukona

NORTH KOHALA

Akoni Pule Highway

Frog Rock

270

Kawaihae Harbor

2

33 miles north of Kona
Kawaihae Rd.

SPENCER BEACH PARK

locked gate →

68   19

to Waimea

MAU'UMAE BEACH
Mauna Kea Resort
KAUNA'OA BEACH

69

32.6 miles north of Kona
guard station

HAPUNA BEACH

WAI'ALEA BAY

1 mile

1.2 miles

SOUTH KOHALA

PUAKO BAY
boat ramp

@ mile 70.4

Puako Rd.

71

30.4 miles north of Kona

PUAKO

end of road

19

HOLOHOLOKAI PARK
PAUOA BAY
MAKAIWA BAY
HONOKA'OPE BAY

The Orchid
Mauna Lani Hotel

73

Mauna Lani Dr.

palms

74

WAIKOLOA VILLAGE

Hilton

a'a lava

75

Outrigger
Kings Shops

heliport

Waikoloa Rd.

6 miles

'ANAEHO'OMALU

76

Waikoloa Beach Dr.
24.5 miles
north of Kona

Pueo Bay

Queen Ka'ahumanu Hwy.

lava flow

Keawaiki Bay

Kaiwi Point

to Kailua-Kona

reddish brown a'a

N

57

Spencer Park

Located off Highway 270 just as it heads north from Highway 19, Spencer Park offers excellent facilities, good swimming, but only fair snorkeling. The best snorkeling is located at the far left along the coast to the south. Watch carefully for big swells or a current off shore because you'll need calm water for safe snorkeling and won't want to get swept south away from the park.

In this elongated park, you'll find multiple restrooms, showers, picnic tables, camping, shade trees and snacks. The sandy beach is a great place for a refreshing swim or for children to play and is somewhat protected much of the year. This is an excellent spot to stop after a snorkel at a nearby site that lacks facilities.

GETTING THERE   Head north on Highway 19 and take the Y to the left as it becomes Highway 270 (rather than right to Waimea). Watch on the left for the sign just north of mile marker 2 (see map, page 57). Head for the parking area at the far left (south). Entry is easy as long as the swell isn't high. Summer mornings are your best bet for calm conditions here.

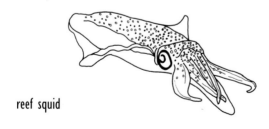

reef squid

58

Sign Language

Any serious snorkeler should bother to learn some basic signs starting with some of the standard Scuba ones: OK — meaning "Are you OK?", which should be answered with another "OK", palm up for "stop", wobbling hand for "problem", thumb down meaning "heading down" (in this case referring to surface diving). This is an essential safety issue making it possible to communicate even if slightly separated or underwater. See a few of the signs below.

It's also a nuisance to take the snorkel out of your mouth every time you want to say "Did you see that moray?" Worse yet is trying to understand your buddy who frantically gestures and mumbles through the snorkel while you play charades. With a frequent snorkeling companion it's fun to develop signs for the creatures you might see. Eel can be indicated by three fingers looking like an E or by a wavy line drawn in the water. Then all you have to do it point and there it is!

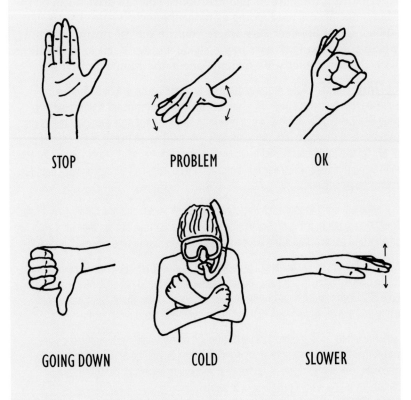

STOP   PROBLEM   OK

GOING DOWN   COLD   SLOWER

Mau'umae Beach

If the 30 passes for the Mauna Kea Beach (Kauna'oa Beach) are in use, consider asking at the same guard station for one of the ten passes to Mau'umae Beach.

Mau'umae Beach is similar to Kauna'oa, but smaller and undeveloped. With no hotel and no facilities, it also has few people, but plenty of fish and coral. There is talk of a hotel at this site, so access may change. If it has, ask for directions at the guard station.

This is a gorgeous, secluded beach with terrific snorkeling and swimming. Just snorkel along the rocks on the left as far as the point. It's calm, clear, and you might even have the whole beach to yourselves if you arrive a bit early. Bathing suits appear optional. No restrooms or showers, but no crowds either. A delightful bay. You can always drive down to the Kauna'oa Beach path to use showers and restrooms after your swim. This requires another hike of about 250 yards.

Alternatively, for showers and restrooms, you can drive north on the Mau'umae access road, going as far as the locked gate. This is the south edge of Spencer Park where you can see the restrooms from where you park. Park here in the shade and walk left to the facilities. It's a shorter, cooler walk than the one to the Kauna'oa facilities.

GETTING THERE   Take Highway 19 north from Kailua-Kona to the Mauna Kea entrance (see area map, page 57). Turn left, then stop at the guard station (see map, page 61). Drive down the hill .4 of a mile, and take the third right turn (just before the road makes a sweeping 90° turn to the left). The third paved road gives the appearance of a hotel service entrance, and has a sign saying "Private Road". Not to worry! In .15 mile along this road, you'll see buildings and lots of service vehicles on your right just before the paving ends.

Continue on, holding to the left through a chain link fence, onto the barely-paved road. Now you are out in the lava countryside. The road is narrow, but not difficult. Cross two small wood plank bridges and pass a private road on the left (see site map, page 61).

At 1/4 mile from where the slightly-paved road started, park along the road, remembering to display your "beach pass" on the dashboard. A small path on the left, near phone pole #22, leads through the shrubs toward the ocean. After about 125 yards, you'll come to a marker saying "Ala Kahaka", where you must turn left or right.

Take the left turn for another 125 yards through some small overhanging trees and you're there. (If you turn right at the T, you'll eventually come to a small rocky cove where a creek comes down—not the best snorkeling access or prospects, but a possibility if you want a private spot to sun).

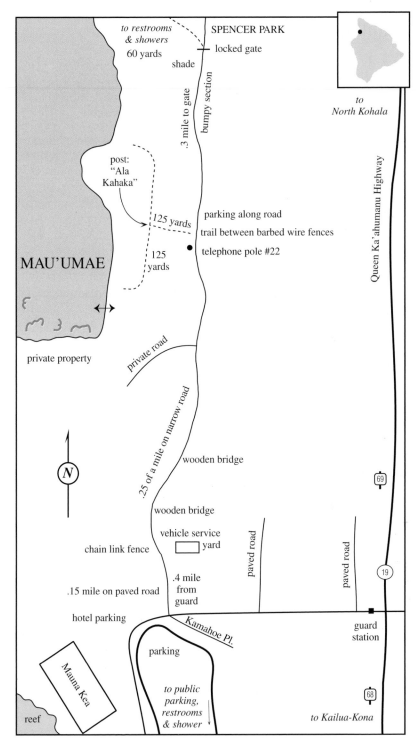

to restrooms
& showers
60 yards

SPENCER PARK

locked gate

shade

.3 mile to gate

bumpy section

post:
"Ala
Kahaka"

125 yards

125
yards

parking along road

trail between barbed wire fences

telephone pole #22

MAU'UMAE

private property

private road

.25 of a mile on narrow road

N

wooden bridge

wooden bridge

vehicle service
yard

chain link fence

.15 mile on paved road

.4 mile
from
guard

paved road

paved road

hotel parking

Mauna Kea

Kamahoe Pl.

parking

to public
parking,
restrooms
& shower

reef

to
North Kohala

Queen Ka'ahumanu Highway

69

19

guard
station

68

to Kailua-Kona

Kauna'oa Beach (Mauna Kea)

In early 1960s, the barren a'a lava fields of Kohala seemed an unlikely and inhospitable spot for hotels. Though the area is fringed with beautiful beaches, they were hard to access unless approached by boat. Only local people visited these beautiful beaches.

This changed forever in 1965, when the first luxury hotel complex along the Kohala Coast was built on beautiful Kauna'oa Beach by L. Rockefeller: the Mauna Kea Beach Resort. This oasis of luxury among the lava fields drew a rich and famous clientele for many years, and has spawned a host of other posh resorts, each larger than the last. The Mauna Kea itself underwent a thorough remodeling in the early 1990s. The beach chosen for this pioneer remains one of the best in Hawai'i, and is often voted best beach in the world.

Kauna'oa Beach has excellent snorkeling and swimming, and is an unforgettable day trip. A beautiful long crescent of soft white coral sand fringed with palms is set off by dark turquoise water. There is plenty of room for hotel guests and visitors alike. The water is usually safe and calm, but the hotel posts signs when warnings are in order—and sometimes when they aren't. Many hotels post perpetual warnings for their own protection.

Snorkel either side out to the point—whichever appears calmest. The left has more coral, but the fish are plentiful on either side. We have seen turtles, eels, and a wide variety of fish.

This is a very protected bay with easy access from the sand. It can get a bit choppy out at the points, but you don't have to swim that far. The excitement starts almost as soon as you enter the water. Come early in the day for calm water and an available parking pass. Excellent restrooms and showers are available near where the path meets the sand.

One word of caution. Small man-of-war jellies sometimes wash up here and can cause a painful sting. We've known people who have been stung, but we have never seen one here ourselves.

The Mauna Kea shines a bright light into the water in the evening to attract manta rays looking for a plankton meal. This is an outstanding place to snorkel with mantas when they show up, Bring your own dive lights (or buy some at WalMart). Snorkel on the north (right) side of the bay out no more than 100 yards to the bright hotel light. Of course, you'll need fairly calm water, but it often gets calm in the early evening—especially in the summer.

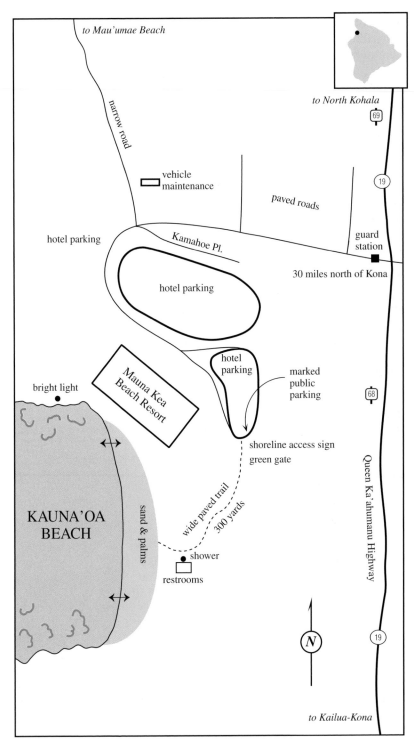

to Mau'umae Beach

narrow road

to North Kohala

69

19

vehicle maintenance

paved roads

hotel parking

guard station

Kamahoe Pl.

30 miles north of Kona

hotel parking

hotel parking

marked public parking

bright light

Mauna Kea Beach Resort

68

shoreline access sign
green gate

KAUNA'OA BEACH

sand & palms

wide paved trail

300 yards

Queen Ka'ahumanu Highway

shower

restrooms

N

19

to Kailua-Kona

63

Swimming with these 8-10' wide mantas is an unforgettable experience! In spite of the size of their mouths, they only eat plankton, not people. If you hit a night when the mantas don't show up, use your dive light to explore a bit along the reef to see a very different set of creatures than during the day. Do be careful to swim around the shallow patch of coral near the beach, and approach the light from the seaward, deep side.

GETTING THERE   Go north on Highway 19 (see area map, page 57), past several major resorts, and on past the turnoff for the town of Waikoloa. Continue past Hapuna Beach, to just past mile marker 69 (32.6 miles north of the Kailua-Kona junction). At the resort entrance, you'll see a guard station (see site map, page 63). Ask for a beach pass (see Passes, page 65). With pass in hand, drive down the hill, curving left, on past the hotel and large parking lots. Enter the very last parking lot. Drive on to the end of the lot, where you'll see marked beach access parking spaces. A wide paved path to the beach begins here. On your left, as you come to the sand, you'll see the first-rate showers and restrooms meticulously maintained by the Mauna Kea.

If no more passes to Kauna'oa Beach are available for the day, ask for a pass to Mau'umae Beach (see page 60).

To see the mantas, go at about 8 pm and tell the guard you're there to see mantas. Park in the hotel lot and walk through the pillars outside the hotel lobby. Continue about 100 yards until you see an orange elevator and take it to G level. Walk out on to the beach, pass the shower, and head for the northern end of the beach. While snorkeling, stay seaward from the coral and lights. The brightly-lit manta area is less than 100 yards out along the north end of the beach.

If you do go at night to snorkel with the mantas, be discreet and respectful of the resort and its paying guests—access at night is a courtesy by the hotel, not a right like daytime beach access.

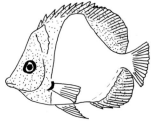

pyramid butterflyfish

Passes

In order to comply with Hawai'ian beach access law, the Mauna Kea Beach Hotel (see page 62) has a unique pass system allowing a limited amount of beach parking.

Thirty prime Kauna'oa Beach parking spaces closest to the beach path are marked beach access, and reserved for pass holders. Parking permit passes for these spaces are issued at the guard station as you enter the resort, on a first-come, first-serve basis. Displayed on your dashboard, they allow you to park for the whole day if desired. As you leave, the guard reclaims them, and the space becomes available for another visitor.

On weekends or holidays, come early to avoid disappointment. Ten passes are also available for Mau'umae Beach, although (as of 2002) you just park alongside a gravel road near the beach access trail. This may change if a new hotel is built in this area.

Another good time to snorkel is late afternoon, when winds sometimes stop completely. Begin your snorkel around 4 or 5 p.m. (when the beach-goers leave) and continue till sundown. You're likely to find access at this hour and will see the creatures of the reef prepare for night.

NOTE: You always have a right to drive down to the head of either trail, drop off or pick up beach goers, and drive back out—one solution if all the passes are in use.

Our compliments go to the Mauna Kea Resort for generously maintaining excellent, clean facilities for showering and changing at the beach. Other resorts would do well to follow their example of providing gracious public access to the beaches that they adjoin, but do not own. A pass system is not perfect, but when run properly seems to work pretty well.

All beaches in Hawai'i are public property, up to the mean high tide line. Land access, however, is often over private property. Large resorts mostly tolerate visitor access if done in a well-mannered way. Blend in, look and act like a guest, and no one cares. Be loud, obnoxious and bothersome, and they'll feel obliged to kick you out. Use common sense—if there are kapu (forbidden) signs posted on private property, respect them.

Hapuna Beach Park

Hapuna is a large, gorgeous public beach, with restrooms, showers, snack shop, grass, plenty of parking and covered picnic tables. This is one of the Big Island's longest, prettiest white sand beaches and is very popular with local folks for picnics and fun. Swimming and snorkeling are both excellent when surf is low and surfing is great when it's high. Hapuna is one of the most dangerous beaches when the surf is up—especially in the winter. Two lifeguard stations provide a chance to check with experts before entering the water.

The surf can be calm as glass in the morning, then pick up quite suddenly around noon. For snorkelers who can't be watching the waves and fish at the same time, this can sneak up on you. During calm conditions, there is snorkeling at both ends of this long beach. Choose according to wave and wind direction. We prefer the north, where we can snorkel against the current, then catch an easy ride returning to the park. While the Hapuna Prince Hotel fronts the far right (north) end of the beach, the beach itself belongs to the Hapuna Beach Park.

When surf is up, try nearby "69" or Kauna'oa for snorkeling, then stop for a picnic or a shower at Hapuna. There is also a 3/4-mile scenic old Hawai'ian trail going north from Hapuna. You may choose to enjoy the scenery and lively social scene here, rather than gamble with heavy waves—especially if you arrive in the winter.

On a calm day, this is an excellent choice for either snorkeling or swimming. We have seen plenty of turtles, interesting scrawled filefish, nearly all of Hawai'i's butterflyfish amidst the healthy lobe and cauliflower coral.

Stay awhile and enjoy the park with its expanse of grass and sand. Plenty of lovely trees line the beach—including kiawe, beach heliotrope and false kamani. It is hard to exaggerate how pleasant Hapuna is—it is one of our favorite well-developed beach parks in all Hawai'i. It is worth a visit just for a picnic if you're not in the mood for a swim, or the surf is up.

GETTING THERE   Go north on Highway 19 past several major resorts, and on past the turnoff for the town of Waikoloa. Soon you'll see a big sign for "Hapuna Beach.", 31.6 miles north of the Kailua-Kona junction (see area map, page 57). This will take you directly to the center of the park, where you'll find plenty of parking and multiple paths down the hill to the sand. Park as far to the north as possible, because you'll need to hike north on the sand for the best snorkeling. Take the path down to the sand and head north on the sand to calm water for snorkeling.

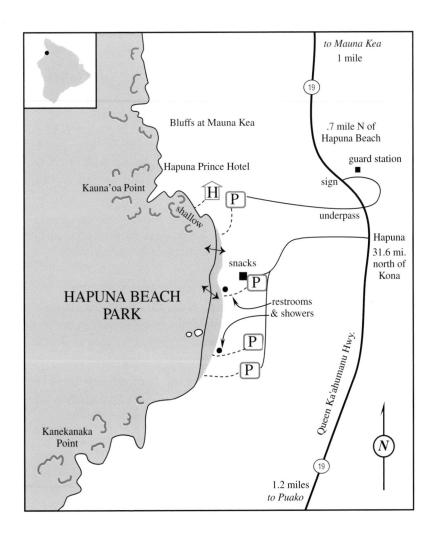

Better yet, try the Hapuna Prince exit, which will bring you to the public parking nearer the best snorkeling. Parking will only be available here if you arrive early. The Hapuna Prince exit is easy to miss because it's on the mauka (mountain) side of the highway. After you pass the Hapuna Beach exit going north, look for the next exit to your right. Take this exit away from the ocean, then follow as it heads back under the highway. You'll need to ask the guard for a pass to park in the public access spaces about a mile from the turnoff. Here, you'll be close to the great snorkeling, but not to any facilities. For showers and restrooms, you'll have to hike south along the beach or drive back to the highway.

Wai'alea Bay (69)

Tucked between Hapuna and Puako, Wai'alea (also called 69, after an old telephone pole formerly located there) is a lovely small oasis hidden by several private homes. Snorkeling is easy and excellent when the sea is calm. This bay offers far more protection from swell than nearby Hapuna. While there are no facilities at the moment, this will eventually change because a public park is being gradually built and houses have been purchased for a pavilion area.

Swimming is best to the right where there's a sandy bottom, but snorkeling is great in the center of the bay—in the area surrounding the small island. This is a chance to see pristine coral and plentiful fish, as well as turtles, all with only a short swim from a sandy beach. This is an excellent choice for either beginners or advanced. Don't miss this wonderful spot.

Stronger swimmers can check out the beautiful coral beyond the point to the right—a large area with plenty to explore when not too rough. In calm weather, we snorkeled all the way to Hapuna Beach.

The left also has an excellent reef that extends far beyond the point and wraps back toward the center of the bay. If you're planning to swim beyond the points, make sure that you go on a calm day. Early mornings are best. You'll definitely want to return.

While the beach still had no facilities as we went to press, the beautiful sandy beach is wide with kukui, ironwood and kiawe trees for plenty of shade. Watch out for one-inch thorns in the sand from these kiawes.

We have seen lots of turtles, a scrawled filefish, huge sailfin tangs, plenty of variety, and even a manta ray out beyond the point. Watch for the big porcupine fish that hang out near shore.

GETTING THERE   From Kailua-Kona, head north on Highway 19, then turn toward Puako on Puako Road (see area map, page 57). Take the first road to the right (toward Hapuna Beach). Drive half a mile (passing the private road), then turn left on a rough dirt road. Drive just .15 of a mile, and park at the end, always holding to the left. If you'd rather not risk your rental car on this very rough road, just hike from the corner. The telephone pole where you turn is #71 (not #69). You can see a large silver-colored gate where the 100-yard path begins. Take this path through the trees and you'll be rewarded with a gorgeous and uncrowded beach, perfect for beginners and advanced alike (see map, page 69). Snorkel directly in front of the path and all around the island. When seas are calm, snorkel beyond either point. We prefer the left. Bring a picnic and stay a while, but take care to remove any trash from this pristine site. Access details will change when the park is developed.

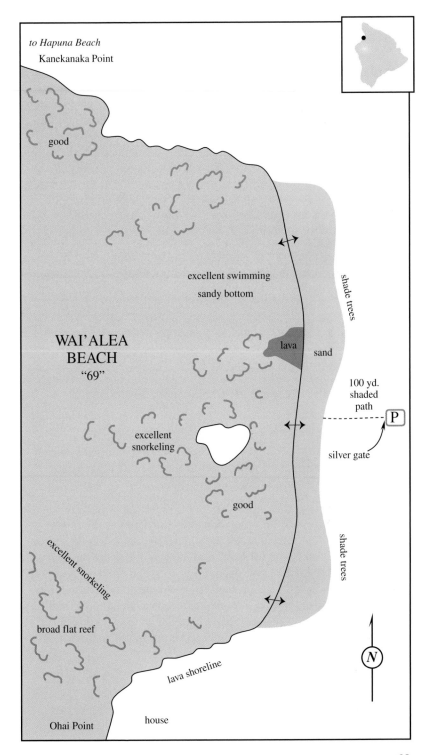

to Hapuna Beach
Kanekanaka Point

good

excellent swimming
sandy bottom

WAI'ALEA
BEACH
"69"

lava

shade trees

sand

100 yd.
shaded
path

P

silver gate

excellent
snorkeling

good

shade trees

excellent snorkeling

broad flat reef

lava shoreline

N

Ohai Point

house

69

Puako Bay (north)

One of the Big Island's excellent, but challenging, snorkeling sites. Puako Bay stretches along four miles of shallow, rocky shoreline. Since the waves can be high and the large inner lagoon very shallow out as far as 200 yards, this can make for a most dangerous entry and exit. Beginning snorkelers would be wise to snorkel here by boat only. There are certainly times when experienced snorkelers can find safe entry at both ends, but beginners should always be wary. Early mornings in the summer will usually make for the safest and most enjoyable snorkeling. High tide or a rising tide is even better. This is a huge area to explore, so allow plenty of time. Watch carefully for offshore currents, usually heading south.

Experienced snorkelers can enter from the boat channel at the north end of the bay. Entry is easy as long as you don't slip on the algae that coats the edge of the ramp. We prefer to enter just to the right instead of using the ramp. Follow the boat channel out until the coral and clarity improve. Be alert for boat traffic, but it's light here and you may see no one in or over the water.

Wander around the reef to your right as far as the outer edge of the reef, taking care to avoid any area with surf. Noon brings wind chop and bigger swells, so come early to best enjoy this broad reef.

When conditions are calm, you can also swim to the left and follow the edge of the reef as far as seems safe. Keep in mind the current tends to head south, so it may be more difficult to snorkel back. You could drift snorkel all four miles to the end of Puako Road, but it's a long hike back to the car.

The large area along the edge of the reef offers some exciting snorkeling when calm. The reef drops off to fifteen to thirty feet, where we have seen turtles, eels, large pufferfish, schools of yellow tang, lots of healthy colorful coral and most of the usual butterfly-fish: raccoon, oval, four-spot, ornate. Even garden eels can be found here, but require good free-diving skills because they're small and emerge from the sand thirty feet deep. You have a chance of sighting a reef shark and other pelagic fish where the water gets deeper off the edge of this large reef. We highly recommend Puako, but only for experienced and cautious snorkelers.

GETTING THERE   From Kailua-Kona, drive north on Highway 19 as it passes the big hotels near the Waikoloa. Continue north until you see the sign to Puako and turn toward the ocean on Puako Road (see area map, page 57). The road will turn back toward your left as it follows the coast south. There are six marked public access trails

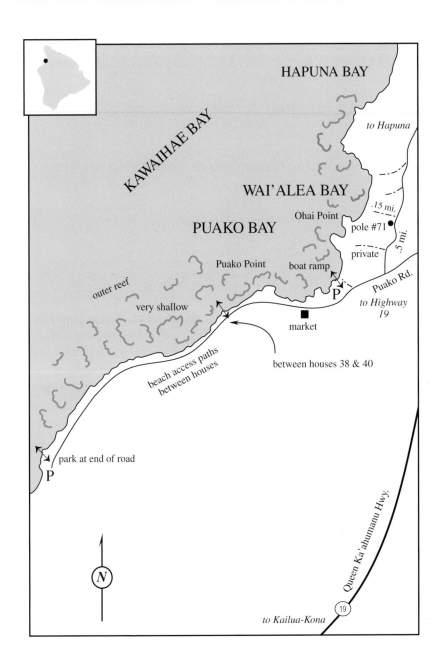

HAPUNA BAY

KAWAIHAE BAY

to Hapuna

WAI'ALEA BAY

Ohai Point

.15 mi.

pole #71

PUAKO BAY

.5 mi.

private

Puako Point

boat ramp

Puako Rd.

P

outer reef

very shallow

to Highway 19

market

beach access paths
between houses

between houses 38 & 40

park at end of road

P

Queen Ka'ahumanu Hwy.

N

19

to Kailua-Kona

71

along this four-mile stretch. Some snorkelers take the access between houses #38 and #40. This nearly hidden path takes you to the middle of the reef, but shouldn't be considered by anyone without experience at Puako.

The first public access at Puako leads to the boat ramp (see site map, page 71), where you will find plenty of parking. Access is easy to the right of the ramp (ramps themselves are slippery). Follow the boat channel out at least 200 yards for the better coral. Then, meander over the reef to the right as long as you can avoid all breaking waves. There's plenty of good snorkeling along the far edge of the reef to the left, but check the current carefully before heading in this direction. Swimming north against the current can be difficult at times.

Puako Bay (south)

Although there are five other public beach accesses (marked by small, sometimes hidden, signs) spread along Puako Road, all are risky because surf conditions can change suddenly and can trap you against a shallow reef. Very experienced snorkelers can head out from the public access path next to house #38, but only when absolutely sure about the conditions.

The safer southern entry is found where Puako Road dead-ends at the south. The south end of the reef is close to shore, angling out as it heads north. Instead of crossing the shallow reef, this entry allows you to skirt around the south end of the reef safely. Stay outside the shallow area and follow the edge of the reef as it heads north (to your right).

Keep in mind that the current here usually heads south, so stay north and you'll have an easier swim back. Place a brightly-colored item on the shore to mark your entry because it's the only safe exit along here. Do NOT attempt to come in over the reef unless you have plenty of local experience. We have seen people stranded on top of the reef waiting for help while in a very vulnerable spot. Not good for you or the reef.

The Puako reef is an excellent one with lots to see including garden eels (down about 30 feet), rays, most of the usual reef fish, and even a reef shark if you're lucky. Come early in the morning (around 8 a.m.) for the best conditions. You're likely to have the whole reef to yourself before any excursions arrive. Wind chop and swells usually pick up late morning, but the afternoon winds often die out completely around 4-5 p.m., so you might catch Puako calm before sunset. This is an excellent time to see the fish darting about, preparing for night.

GETTING THERE   From Kailua-Kona, drive north on Highway 19 as it passes the big hotels near the Waikoloa. Continue north until you see the sign to Puako and turn toward the ocean (see map, page 57). The road will turn back toward your left as it follows the coast south. There are six public access trails (see site map, page 71).

The first access heads to the Puako boat ramp, then you'll pass short paths between houses. Continue to the end of the road and park on the dirt just off the end of the road. Look over the spots that allow access between the lava and pick whichever look easiest. This is just a stone's throw from your car. It's important to leave something colorful to mark your entry because this is the only place for a safe exit—particularly if swells pick up, which they usually do by noon. Do NOT attempt to swim in over the shallow reef.

High tide makes this entrance even easier, although it isn't essential. If conditions are rough, don't even think of swimming here.

No facilities here. There's also little sand along this bay, just a wide shallow reef that's great for checking the tidepools, but dangerous for swimming. The deeper water beyond the reef has excellent snorkeling all along this broad bay. When calm, Puako is a popular destination for excursions. Beginners should stick with excursions that access only the outer edge of the reef.

saddleback butterflyfish

Pauoa Bay (The Orchid)

The popular Orchid at Mauna Lani has created an elegant tropical oasis surrounding the small, pretty white-sand beach on Pauoa Bay.

This is an easy place to snorkel, but the coral and fish have declined in recent years. The rocky areas outside the inner bay are better for snorkeling than swimming, because of sharp rocks, coral and sometimes sea urchins in shallow water areas. Fresh water runoff is common here, giving an oily look to the water in places (see Doctor my Eyes, page 141).

Brown algae has covered much of the coral recently. Still, there are fish to see such as the Picasso triggerfish—our cover fish, and one of our favorites in Hawai'i. The small bay is well-protected and not very deep, perfect for beginning snorkelers. More experienced snorkelers will prefer to swim much further out and toward the south. Or better yet, snorkel fabulous Makaiwa Bay near the Mauna Lani Bay Hotel to the south.

GETTING THERE   The turnoff for The Orchid at Mauna Lani is easy to find between mile 73 and 74 on Highway 19 (see area map, page 57). Three different public access paths are available within the large Mauna Lani property. Hotel guests can take a shuttle to any of the beaches, but public parking is less convenient. The three lots are located at Holoholokai Park, across from the small store, and south near Honoka'ope Beach.

To snorkel at Pauoa Bay, follow the signs and park in the lot at Holoholokai Beach County Park, which is the next beach north along the coast road from the hotel (see site map, page 75).

After turning toward the Mauna Lani from Highway 19, bear right at the roundabout and take North Kaniku Drive, then take another right when you near The Orchid. This road has a sign and will lead you to the public park. It's a pretty spot for a picnic, with new showers and restrooms. The park also has plenty of grass, picnic tables and is an attractive spot for a picnic, however, the coast is lava with no beach in front.

To get to Pauoa Bay, take a quarter-mile hike south on a chunky lava path along the water. You'll quickly see why shoes are required—not just flip-flops. This is a sharp, a'a lava path with no shade! Follow the coast south, watching out for stray golf balls. As you near the hotel, choose a spot to enter the water. It's actually easier to enter the water at the alternative entry point shown on the map, across from the pool, rather than walking as far as the hotel swimming entry. Snorkel out beyond the protected swimming cove. Visibility improves are you head away from the beach. When seas permit, snorkel across the broad reef to the south. Just be sure the offshore currents aren't too strong because those can carry you south and make your return difficult.

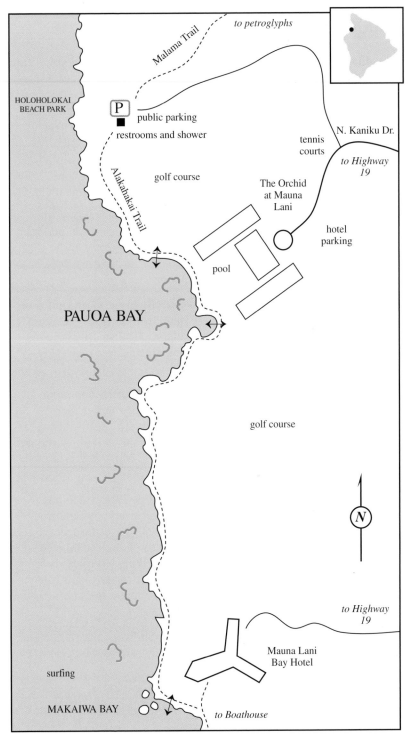

to petroglyphs

Malama Trail

HOLOHOLOKAI
BEACH PARK

P public parking
restrooms and shower

N. Kaniku Dr.

tennis courts

to Highway 19

golf course

Alakahakai Trail

The Orchid at Mauna Lani

hotel parking

pool

PAUOA BAY

golf course

N

to Highway 19

surfing

Mauna Lani Bay Hotel

MAKAIWA BAY

to Boathouse

Makaiwa Bay (Mauna Lani Bay Hotel)

Less than half a mile south of the Mauna Lani Bay Hotel, you'll find one of the Big Island's best snorkeling reefs. The area straight in front of the hotel is mostly too shallow with too much swell for safe snorkeling, but the reef to the south is just about perfect and tends to be calm. Snorkeling access is very easy from the sandy beach. Public parking, however, is well-hidden and requires about a 3/4-mile hike to the beach. The snorkeling here tends to be calm all day, but wind chop in the afternoon can reduce visibility. Late afternoon sometimes brings calm again, although is rarely as clear as morning.

Snorkel out from the Mauna Lani Beach Club (just south of the Mauna Lani Terrace) and you'll find a large horseshoe-shaped reef stretching about 100 yards from shore. If you're staying at the Mauna Lani Bay Hotel or the Terrace condos, it's an easy walk meandering through the historic fish ponds.

The reef here is excellent and uncrowded. Beginners can find safe and easy snorkeling near shore with entry from a calm, protected, sandy beach. More experienced snorkelers will love cruising the whole area out to the far edge of the reef. Head toward the buoy, then just as far beyond it to see the outer reef.

Snorkeling addicts will also enjoy heading to the left and around Mauna Lani Point (in calm conditions only, since this is more exposed). For a great one-way snorkel, follow the coast south as far as seems comfortable. There are several places to exit along the golf course. Poke between the little fingers of lava. Most of this stretch is about five to twenty feet deep.

A strong swimmer can go as far as Honoka'ope Bay, which has recently been opened to the public. If you get tired of swimming, just scramble up to the Ala Kahakai Trail that's never far from the sea along the golf course. The trail is smooth enough to take you back to the Beach Club even if your feet are bare. No rough lava once you're on the trail. If you feel like collecting golf balls, there are plenty in five-foot deep water along the edge of the lava near the oceanside golf holes south of Mauna Lani Point.

The Beach Club restaurant is open 11 to 4. Showers are available at the beach. Showers and restrooms are also back at public parking.

GETTING THERE From Highway 19, turn toward the Mauna Lani Hotel on Mauna Lani Drive (see area map, page 57). Continue straight at the round-about for another 1.5 miles, then take a left on Pauoa Road for 1.1 mile. Turn right at the small sign

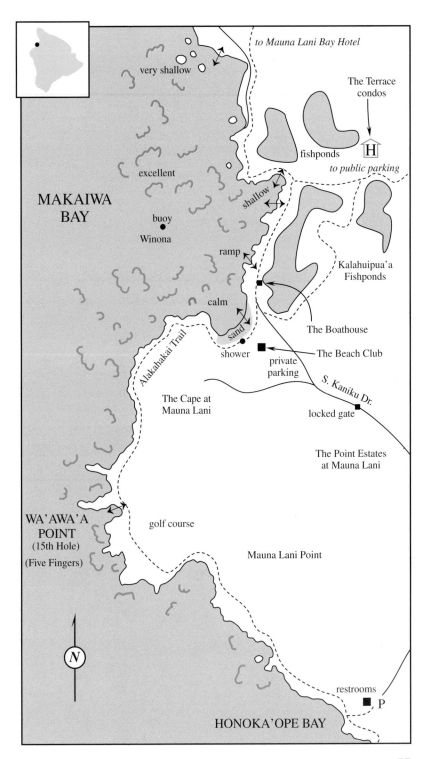

to Mauna Lani Bay Hotel

very shallow

The Terrace condos

fishponds

to public parking

MAKAIWA BAY

excellent

shallow

buoy
Winona

ramp

Kalahuipua'a Fishponds

calm

sand

The Boathouse

shower

The Beach Club

private parking

S. Kaniku Dr.

Alakahakai Trail

The Cape at Mauna Lani

locked gate

The Point Estates at Mauna Lani

WA'AWA'A POINT
(15th Hole)
(Five Fingers)

golf course

Mauna Lani Point

N

restrooms
P

HONOKA'OPE BAY

across from the general store into the small (19-car) parking area with shower, restrooms and shade trees.

The trail starts to the right of the restrooms and wanders 3/4 of a mile through the Mauna Lani property (see map, page 77). You'll meander through the Kalahuipua'a Fishponds holding fish within the traditional sluice gates. You may see fish jumping in the ponds and quail walking on the path—a very lovely walk. When you get to the water, enter directly in front if tide is high enough for clearance and water calm. Otherwise, continue walking left (south) to the sandy beach for the easiest entry.

Even at low tide, the boat channel is also deep enough for easy entrance. Of course, the sandy beach entry is easiest of all. Snorkel out about 100 yards and continue to the right (north) to explore this excellent reef. You'll see a buoy or boat halfway to the outer edge of the reef. Depth varies from about five to twenty-five feet. Be alert for boat traffic because there are seldom many snorkelers here. Don't miss this excellent site. You'll want to come again.

If you'd like a detailed map of the whole property (with interesting narrative), stop at security on your way in (along the right side of Mauna Lani Drive) and ask for "View into the Past."

Mauna Lani Terrace

The Mauna Lani Terrace, adjoining the historic Kalahuipua'a fishponds, is part of the spacious 3,200 acre Mauna Lani Resort. There are few properties in Hawaii that are set so close to excellent beaches, swimming and snorkeling.

The authors, after years of searching for a place to live in Hawai'i with just the right combination of pleasant weather, tropical surroundings, excellent year-round swimming and snorkeling within walking distance (of course!), chose the Mauna Lani Terrace. For more information, see

http://www.snorkelguides.com/terrace.htm

which has full information and pictures.

Honoka'ope Bay

This small black-sand beach now has good public access with twenty parking spaces and restrooms. No showers were available when we last snorkeled, but the landscaping sprinklers nearly did the trick. The road has recently been completed, so perhaps showers will be next.

The bay offers easy entry except for the small chunks of rock and coral as you step into the water. Enter anywhere along this small beach. Snorkel out beyond the point to the left when calm. You can snorkel to the right although will find mostly rubble near the beach. While not nearly as good as Makaiwa Beach, at least the walk from car to sand is short. A very long snorkel will take you to the beach at Makaiwa Bay.

The road is only open from sunrise to sunset, but the gate will always swing open when you depart, so you won't be trapped.

GETTING THERE   Head north on Highway 19 to the Mauna Lani sign (see area map, page 57). Heading toward the hotel, you'll come to a large roundabout. Here you'll need to head left on South Kaniku Drive. Pass the King's Trail (the wide straight trail), then turn left on Honoka'ope Place. Stop at the guard house and ask for public access parking. Follow this road to the end (.7 of a mile) where you'll find a parking lot with restrooms. The beach is only 100 yards away (see site map, page 75).

trumpetfish

'Anaeho'omalu Bay (north)

The northern edge of 'Anaeho'omalu Bay (in front of the Outrigger Hotel) offers excellent snorkeling if you don't mind swimming out a ways past the generally poor visibility near shore. Head out from anywhere near the water sports shop. Entry is easy from the sand, but you won't see much near shore if swell has stirred up the sand. Continue till the water gets clearer and the coral large and healthy. There is a wide area to explore on your right since the reef extends to the waves breaking against the far edge (somewhat in line with the two points). Avoid any areas of breaking surf, but you should be able to find plenty of excellent, calm snorkeling. Water depth is good (5-20 feet) with large coral heads and plenty of fish.

We prefer to roam the area on the north close to the far edge of the reef. It's a long swim, but much better snorkeling than the shallower areas near shore, which have poor visibility.

Showers are available near the water sports building, at the north end of the Outrigger. There is a hotel parking lot available up the hill with an easy walkway down to the beach. If it's full, you'll have to park about 500 yards to the north at the nearest public access. It's an even longer walk from the public parking south of the hotel.

GETTING THERE   From Highway 19, take the turnoff to the Waikoloa hotels (see map, page 57). Head toward the hotels and follow the street as it curves to the right after the Outrigger Hotel. Either park in the north hotel parking lot, or follow the coast north until you see the public parking lot next to the anchialine pool path to the ocean. Turn left at the path along the water and continue about 500 yards south to 'Anaeho'omalu Bay. Begin your snorkel in front of the water sports office near the water.

'Anaeho'omalu Bay (south)

The public park at 'Anaeho'omalu Bay (usually called "A" Bay) is pretty, calm and very popular. Entry is very easy all along this white sand beach and you can snorkel around scattered boulders and some coral heads in 5-10' deep water. Because of the large number of people and boats, the coral has taken a beating here. The visibility is usually limited, due to the sandy bottom getting stirred up.

The crowds and low visibility may put some folks off. Still, most people are taken by the wide and pretty beach with plenty of palms for shade. It's certainly a good place for children and beginners. There are enough fish to make it interesting for everyone. Snorkel just about anywhere weaving among the coral heads.

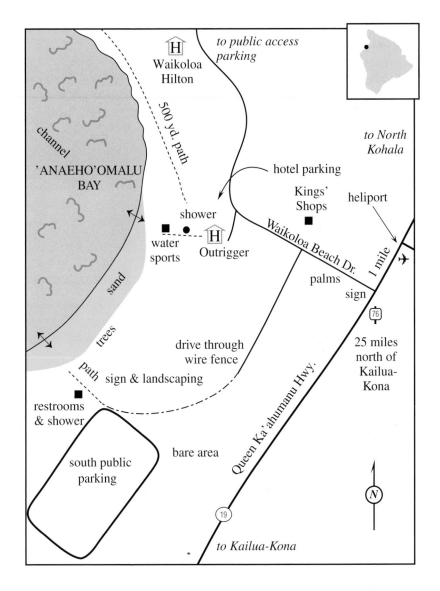

The parking area is gravel, but the short path emerges into a lovely park with showers, restrooms, landscaping and a huge bay full of boats, people, sports of all kinds, plus patchy coral and pretty fish.

GETTING THERE   At the 76 mile marker on Highway 19 (see area map, page 57), take the turnoff toward the big resorts (including the Royal Waikoloan). This intersection (Waikoloa Beach Drive) is 24.5 miles from the Kailua-Kona junction. When you see the Kings' Shops on your right, take a sharp left just across from the shops.

Continue on, through an open gate, and drive until you reach the very last parking area near the water. The short path emerges at the south end of 'Anaeho'omalu Bay.

81

North Kona area

North Kona, with a large number of snorkeling sites, stretches from north of the Keahole Airport to south of Kailua-Kona. While there are a few resorts in the north (such as the Kona Coast Village and the Four Seasons/Hualalai), most of the land here is still undeveloped and much of it is bare black lava from Hualalai's last eruption. There are a number of beautiful bays surrounded by white sand and palm trees where the a'a lava gives way to an oasis. The road to Kekaha Kai Park (just north of the airport) offers access to three of these lovely bays.

Nearly all these North Kona snorkeling sites require a hike from the highway, a park, or from public parking located away from the beaches. We will continue with our counter-clockwise listing of the attractive and accessible snorkeling sites. In the northern section of the North Kona district, you'll find plenty of beaches (many of them large), but seldom visible or accessible from the highway.

Further south in this district, near Kailua-Kona, there are plenty of hotels, condos, timeshares, homes, restaurants and shopping. Kailua is the Big Island's most developed city. It has no large beaches, and is mostly a rough lava shoreline with a few scattered small sandy beaches. This lack of sand actually makes for better and clearer snorkeling, although finding a safe entry and exit can often be a challenge.

There are plenty of small coves scattered throughout the area and conditions are sometimes calmer here than anywhere else on the island. Kahalu'u Beach, with its breakwater can even be calm during a big storm when nearly all other beaches on the island are too rough. There's an abundance of sun in Kona, with little rain or wind, so it can be quite warm in the summer (especially September). Few snorkelers complain about this.

While people do snorkel directly off the rugged lava coast along Kailua-Kona, we recommend that most snorkelers stick with the easier beaches, in case conditions change. Even a small swell can make your exit difficult when the lava is sharp.

Cool fresh water seeps into the bays along much of this coast, so don't be surprised to swim into some surprisingly cool patches. Water temperature will alternate as you swim. Fresh water will also affect the visibility by making the water blurry now and then. No problem—just swim a ways and it will clear up. Often you need to swim away from the beach to reach the warmer, clearer water.

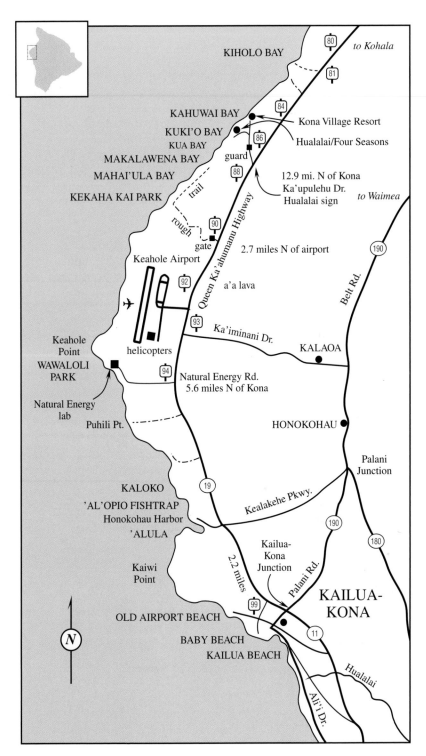

KIHOLO BAY

80

81

to Kohala

KAHUWAI BAY

84

Kona Village Resort

KUKI'O BAY

86

Hualalai/Four Seasons

KUA BAY

MAKALAWENA BAY

guard

88

12.9 mi. N of Kona
Ka'upulehu Dr.
Hualalai sign

to Waimea

MAHAI'ULA BAY

KEKAHA KAI PARK

trail

190

rough

90

2.7 miles N of airport

gate

Keahole Airport

a'a lava

92

Queen Ka'ahumanu Highway

Belt Rd.

93

Ka'iminani Dr.

KALAOA

Keahole
Point

helicopters

WAWALOLI
PARK

94

Natural Energy Rd.
5.6 miles N of Kona

Natural Energy
lab

Puhili Pt.

HONOKOHAU

Palani
Junction

KALOKO

'AL'OPIO FISHTRAP

19

Honokohau Harbor

Kealakehe Pkwy.

190

'ALULA

180

Kaiwi
Point

Kailua-
Kona
Junction

2.2 miles

Palani Rd.

KAILUA-
KONA

OLD AIRPORT BEACH

99

BABY BEACH

11

KAILUA BEACH

Hualalai

Ali'i Dr.

N

Kiholo Bay

This gorgeous oasis surrounding a shallow bay requires a long hike from the road, but is a delightful spot for a secluded picnic, swim or snorkel. The bay is mostly quite shallow (less than fifteen feet), and very calm. Snorkeling is quite good (not great), but the beauty of this bay is worth the hike. Fish here are mostly tiny (like a fish nursery), while the larger ones are skittish. Turtles seem entirely unafraid and we have seen as many as twenty of them—making the hike well worth the effort. Beginners who prefer shallow water will really appreciate Kiholo Bay because it's only 5-10' deep with the easiest entry possible from a sandy beach.

The large bay is beautiful with scenic views of the Kohala Mountains. You'll find a few empty houses, picnic table, and a 4WD road, but seldom any people in sight. This is a lovely area to explore, with reliably calm water for a quick dip or snorkel. Other than the picnic table, there are no facilities here.

For a distant glimpse of pretty Kiholo Bay, stop at the scenic vista along Highway 19 at mile marker 82.

GETTING THERE You'll need to park along Highway 19 on either side of mile marker 81 (see area map, page 83). Head toward the water and you'll find the path running toward your left (see site map, page 85). The path will wind back toward the water and continue for half a mile to the first gate. Then you'll need to hike another quarter mile to the second gate. At this point, walk around the closed gate, and head right about 200 yards to the water. You'll pass an old house on your left and a water tower to the right. While the beach is mostly pebbles, the water here is calm and shallow. Entry is very easy making this a great site for beginners.

Most of the way you'll be hiking on an old 4WD road, however, cars can't enter due to the piles of fallen trees placed in the road to prevent access. On the hike, watch for the green sand on the path. It's left over from Hualalai's last eruption.

needlefish

84

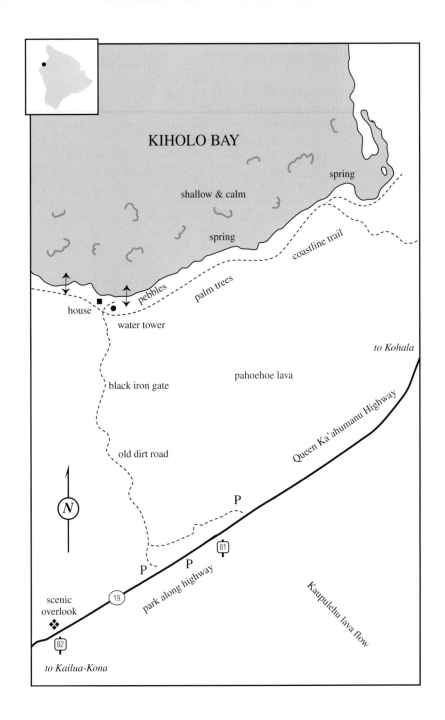

KIHOLO BAY

shallow & calm

spring

spring

coastline trail

pebbles

palm trees

house

water tower

to Kohala

black iron gate

pahoehoe lava

old dirt road

Queen Ka'ahumanu Highway

N

P

P

81

P

park along highway

19

scenic
overlook

Kaupulehu lava flow

82

to Kailua-Kona

85

Kahuwai Bay (Kona Village)

The elegantly-casual Kona Village Resort surrounds calm and lovely Kahuwai Bay, where snorkeling is excellent when conditions are good—especially in the mornings. Finding public access is the hard part. Come early (before 9) and you may have the whole bay to yourself. Later in the day, the water tends to be choppy and you'll find more people, boats and kayaks. Late afternoon (4 or 5) often brings calm water again, but will be less clear with stirred-up sand.

Snorkeling is easy with entry anywhere along the sandy beach. To get to the far north side, either snorkel across the bay (plenty of clearance over the reef) or walk on the sand to the far northern end. There's plenty to see in the middle of the bay, but the best snorkeling is near the lava rocks along the northern end of the beach. When extra calm, you can even continue past the northern point to find a tiny black-sand beach. Turtles are common at Kahuwai and manta rays often wander through this bay.

GETTING THERE   Heading north on Highway 19, go 12.9 miles north of the Kailua-Kona Junction (see area map, page 83). When you see the Kekaha Kai Park sign, watch for the next exit on your left, then turn toward the ocean on Ka'upulehu Dr. Go .9 of a mile to the guard station, where you may need to insist on your right to park in their public access spaces. At the next Y, the right heads to the resort, while the left heads to the employee parking area, where there are 13 public parking spaces. Nothing attractive about this bare gravel parking lot with no shade.

You'll find a half-mile long path to the beach beginning just to the left of the fence. Restrooms and a shower are located on the right of this unshaded path. The path emerges at the southern end of the bay on the border between Kona Coast Resorts and the Four Seasons. There is lava in front, so you will need to hike a bit further to the right to get to an easy entry point from the sand. Explore anywhere within the outer half of the bay where the edge of the reef drops off, but the snorkeling is a bit better on the north side of the bay toward the rocks.

While the Kona Village Resort itself has guest parking with a path much closer to the north end of the bay, none of that is available for public access. Kona Village Resort gets our no-star award for public access attitude—they make it as difficult, distant and unattractive as possible, presumably to maintain near-exclusive beach access for their guests. It would be easy to locate the parking closer to the water, and have a paved, shaded path. As it is, we imagine some folks go ahead and park in the main hotel lot.

Or, for a prettier access path, our preference is to go to the Hualalai/Four Seasons public access parking and walk north along the beach path (see page 87). This takes off from Hualalai's northern public parking lot. There is also a southern access, which is an attractive boardwalk path that crosses a small bridge leading to a shallow bay. This has difficult snorkeling access. See our directions on page 88 for Kuki'o Bay north.

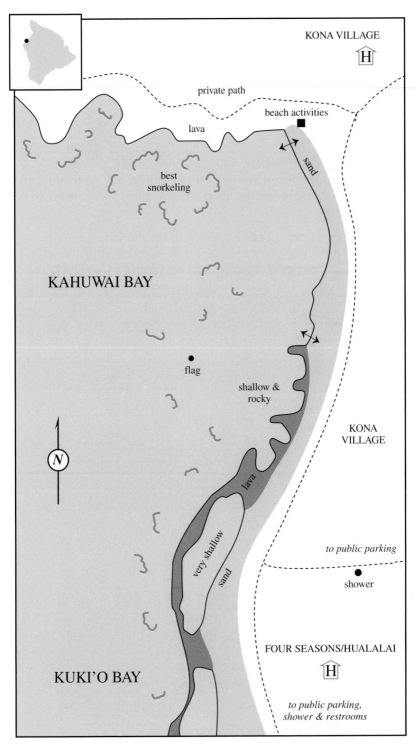

KONA VILLAGE

Ĥ

private path

beach activities

lava

sand

best
snorkeling

KAHUWAI BAY

flag

shallow &
rocky

KONA
VILLAGE

lava

N

very shallow

sand

to public parking

shower

KUKI'O BAY

FOUR SEASONS/HUALALAI

Ĥ

to public parking,
shower & restrooms

87

Kuki'o Bay (north)

You'll have to come early if you want to park at the Four Seasons/Hualalai, due to the few public access parking spots. You'll need to ask at the gatehouse for visitor passes, then hang them in your car and park in one of the ten designated spots. The ocean here is rough with lots of lava along the edge. The man-made lagoon provides easy snorkeling for guests only—perfect for a beginner. This is the kind of enhanced swimming pool we'd like to have at home—salt water, complete with lots of colorful fish. Several other small natural lagoons line the shore. All are too shallow for good snorkeling, but fun for little kids.

The best snorkeling is found by hiking along the walkway to the north, where you can enter the water at Kahuwai Bay in front of the Kona Village Resort. Or continue walking north on the sand to the far northern edge of the bay. On a hot day, swimming across the bay may be easier and more fun.

GETTING THERE   From Kailua-Kona, go north on Highway 19, then turn makai (toward the ocean) on Ka'upulehu Drive (see area map, page 83). Get a pass from the guard station and head toward the Hualalai parking lot to find public parking spaces at the southwest corner of the lot near a yellow fire hydrant. From here, go straight on the path (not right) for about 150 yards to a T. Go right at the T and you will come to a Y. Either direction will take you to the beach. At the beach, take the path along the coast to your right (see map, page 87 for the snorkeling entries).

Beginners or children might want to practice their skills in the very shallow, enclosed pools in front of the Four Seasons/Hualalai Resort. Their deeper man-made snorkeling pool is reserved for guests only.

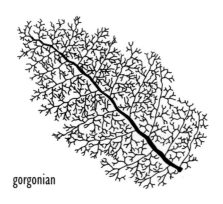

gorgonian

Kuki'o Bay (south)

Public access is easy and this southern portion of Kuki'o Bay is an excellent spot for a picnic, but the water is quite shallow for either swimming or snorkeling. You might want to come here to relax on the sand after snorkeling further north. Low shade trees and picnic tables are available on the sand, with excellent showers and restrooms located near the parking lot. This is a gorgeous beach, quite secluded, and worth another stop if you're out this way.

GETTING THERE From Kailua-Kona, head north on Highway 19, then turn toward the ocean on Ka'upulehu Drive (see area map, page 83). At the far southern end of Hualalai, you'll find a public parking lot with a pretty 250-yard path to the sand. Showers and restrooms are available near the parking lot. Picnic tables and shade trees are available on the beach. This path crosses a little bridge south of the resort rather than leading through the Four Seasons/Hualalai Resort.

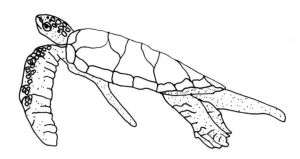

green sea turtle

Makalawena Bay

This picturesque bay is secluded and surrounded by low sand dunes. While the snorkeling isn't the best in the area, the bay does tend to be much calmer than Kekaha Kai State Park (previously called Kona Coast State Park). It's a fairly long, hot hike over chunks of rough lava. The first part of the hike to Mahai'ula Bay is easy enough, but you'll find the path then gets worse (lava chunks the size of golf balls) and very bare, so bring plenty of water and a hat if you plan to hike this far. Wear sturdy shoes too. There are no facilities other than portapotties, but people love Makalawena Bay for its seclusion and pretty beach. Snorkeling is good and swimming is excellent, although you do have to watch out for rocks. At Makalawena, you're likely to see turtles, but visibility isn't great due to all that lovely sand. Still, it's a gorgeous turquoise bay with fine, soft white sand and tiny secluded coves nestled near the dunes.

GETTING THERE   Follow the instructions to Kekaha Kai State Park 2.7 miles north of the Keahole Airport entrance (see area map, page 83). Park in the dirt lot on your left when you approach the beach (page 91) and see a blocked-off 4WD dirt road crossing the entrance road. Hike on this 4WD road north. You will pass Mahai'ula Bay (at about 3/8 of a mile) before the path gets distinctly rougher and hotter. Hike another 45 minutes on this rougher lava. When you see sand dunes, watch for Makalawena Bay and pick your spot. Several trails cross over the dunes to the bay. You'll probably have a beach to yourselves. There are no facilities here except for picnic tables and portapotties. The hike is only about a mile from the parking area, but is a very slow and hot mile.

Mahai'ula Bay

Nearly as pretty as Makalawena, Mahai'ula Bay requires a much shorter and easier hike. It too has few visitors. This is a delightful little oasis with a coarse salt-and-pepper sand beach, shade trees, no facilities, but relatively calm water. While the snorkeling isn't exciting at this sandy beach, it's easy and you will see some fish and probably turtles. It's an excellent swimming and sunning spot within easy hiking from Kekaha Kai State Park. Definitely worth the hike. Mahai'ula Bay seems more protected than either Makalawena or Kekaha Kai, so this is an excellent choice for beginners. And lovely enough to be worth the hike even for those who don't want to get in the water.

GETTING THERE   Follow the instructions to Kekaha Kai State Park 2.7 miles north of the Keahole Airport entrance (see map, page 83). As you approach the beach, park early in the public lot on the left where a 4WD road crosses the entrance road. Park here and

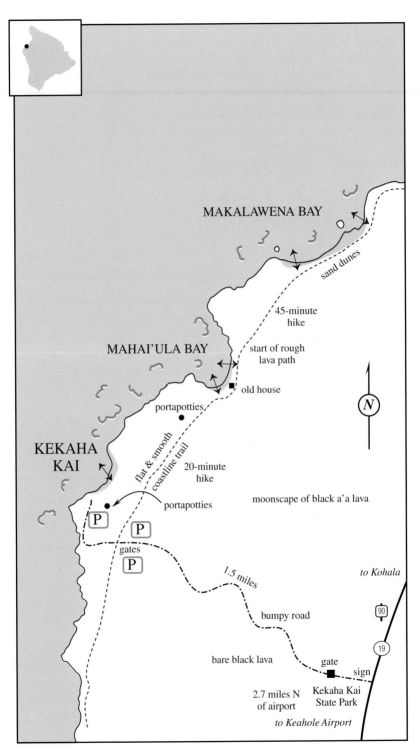

MAKALAWENA BAY

sand dunes

45-minute
hike

MAHAI'ULA BAY

start of rough
lava path

old house

N

portapotties

KEKAHA
KAI

flat & smooth
coastline trail

20-minute
hike

moonscape of black a'a lava

portapotties

P

P

gates

P

1.5 miles

to Kohala

90

bumpy road

19

bare black lava

gate

sign

2.7 miles N
of airport

Kekaha Kai
State Park

to Keahole Airport

hike north on the blocked-off 4WD road (see map, page 91). Hike the old road 3/8 of a mile north until you come to multiple paths heading left to the pretty bay with an old house on the sand. This path is fairly smooth, but heads out across bare lava making it a hot trek in the summer. You may see wild white goats wending their way across the lava like mystical heat-induced hallucinations. What do they eat?

There are portapotties to the left of the trail and you'll see an old house as the trail approaches the bay. The south end of Mahai'ula Bay is reached from a trail that's only about 100 yards past the portapotties. There's plenty of seclusion available under the trees scattered around the low hills of sand.

Kekaha Kai State Park

Previously called Kona Coast State Park, the entrance to Kekaha Kai provides access to three lovely beaches. The long, bumpy access road takes you slowly across the moonscape to Kakaha Kai, which is large, pretty and still fairly undeveloped. Sometimes the swells are quite high in the winter, however, the reef is large and offers some protection when surf isn't too high.

Snorkel almost anywhere along the right half of the beach. There are plenty of coral ridges, so watch for clearance and incoming waves. You won't want to get caught between the coral and a wave.

Kekaha Kai Beach is large and we have had the whole place to ourselves—especially in the early morning before the fishermen arrive. We particularly enjoy the sea turtles here. The water is usually choppy and a bit murky, but still very interesting with plenty of good-sized pelagic fish. This is a popular spot for local fishing and you may see someone catch an octopus. If the water here seems too rough, consider hiking further to Mahai'ula Bay or Makalawena Bay, both of which offer more protection from swells and far better swimming. Beginners should consider Mahai'ula, which is much easier and safer.

GETTING THERE   Take Highway 19 north 2.7 miles past the Keahole Airport entrance (see area map, page 83). Watch carefully for a small road to the left, 9.7 miles from the Kailua-Kona Junction. There is a sign, but it's easy to miss. Follow a 1.5-mile long rough road built across rugged and bare lava heading toward the ocean—actually an interesting approach over moon-like terrain (see site map, page 91). Some people find the road too daunting, so don't bother if you hate lots of ruts. This is slow going at best. Don't show up on a Wednesday or before 9:00 a.m., because the gate will be locked and it would be a very long hot hike. No facilities are provided at the moment—other than ample parking and some portapotties. There is no water available.

Motion Sickness

Motion sickness (such as seasickness, carsickness or airsickness) is a minor inner ear disorder which can really cut into your pleasure on the water, on long, curvy road trips or in choppy air. Fortunately, motion sickness is quite controllable these days. All it takes is a little advance planning to turn a potentially miserable experience into a normal, fun one. Don't let old fears keep you from great water adventures anymore.

Mel can get seasick just by vividly imagining a rocking boat, so he has personally tried just about every remedy. These field trials are a messy business, so we'll spare you the details, and just pass on what really works in our experience.

Forget the wrist pressure-point bands — they don't do the job for anyone we've ever met. You might as well put them in the closet along with your ultrasonic pest repeller, in our opinion.

The most effective remedy we've found so far is Meclizine, a pill available by prescription only. It works perfectly for Mel with no noticeable side effects. Alcohol can apparently interact with it to make you drowsy, though Mel has had a beer on excursions without falling asleep.

We learned about Meclizine when Jon Carroll, a columnist in the San Francisco Chronicle, reported that it had sufficed for him in 15-25' swells on the way to Antarctica. If it does the job there, it should handle all but the most radical of snorkeling excursions. It's always worked for us.

An over-the-counter alternative is Benadryl usually used as a decongestant. It can also be effective against motion sickness. Ginger is also claimed to be effective. As much as we enjoy ginger, we cannot substantiate that it helps at all.

Use these medicines carefully and only after consulting your doctor. In some cases, you must avoid alcohol, other drugs or diving, since these medications can produce drowsiness.

Kekaha Kai State Park has an excellent kayak entry point as you walk out on the sand to your right and watch for a good break in the reef. This is a popular spot to set off to explore the beautiful bays to the north. For kayaking, stay north of the old lifeguard station—now just a square of concrete in the sand.

Wawaloli Beach Park

There are several beach access spots in this park, but none leads to safe snorkeling or swimming. The combination of rough waves and lava shoreline make it more suitable for surfers. It does have a shower, restrooms, and some trees, so you might want to stop here for the facilities. The reason for the big surf here is that the ocean floor drops off to about 2,000 feet right near the coast. This is a pretty and interesting place to visit even if you don't go in the water.

GETTING THERE Heading north on Highway 19 from the Kailua-Kona Junction, go 5.6 miles (see map, page 83). Then turn makai (toward the ocean) where you will find the Natural Energy Lab of Hawai'i. As you approach the water, a Y becomes a dirt road on your left leading to the good surfing. The right heads .3 of a mile to Wawaloli Beach Park, where you will find several beach access signs. The energy lab is located here because of the extremely steep drop-off, so the water is 2,000 feet deep close to shore. And usually very rough.

Kaloko-Honokohau Park

This pretty park down a dirt road offers picnic tables and restrooms, but no drinking water or showers. The park has a large fishpond and historic relics, so is interesting, but not really a good snorkeling destination. The shore is entirely lava and the waves are usually large. The entrance road is also narrow and quite bumpy, so you may not want to drive here in a rental car.

If you go, check out one of Hawai'i's few protected wetland habitats and enjoy the tidepools, but stay away from the open ocean unless you hit extremely calm water conditions. Any entry will be over rough lava with the possibility of larger surf kicking up suddenly. This is a site best reached by boat.

GETTING THERE The entrance is an easily-missed dirt road off Highway 19 (see area map, page 83). It is just south of Hina Lani (where Costco is located) and north of the Honokohau Harbor (see map, page 97). Take the narrow, bumpy dirt road toward the ocean for .7 of a mile and park at the end. This is probably not the best road for rental cars. While the drive is arid, there is plenty of greenery when you arrive at this oasis of a park. Worth a stop, but not for a snorkel or swim.

rectangular triggerfish

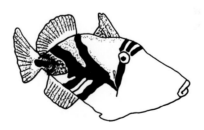

Picasso triggerfish

Honokohau Harbor (north)

Just north of the harbor, you can head to the beach, where (with a little effort) you will find a pretty beach with a shallow, protected cove. High tide is essential for snorkeling and you'll want to swim out a bit for some clearance. This is a great spot for little kids to wade, but too shallow for good swimming. There are no facilities out here, but restrooms and showers are available back at the harbor.

GETTING THERE   From Highway 19, take the Honokohau Harbor exit (see area map, page 83 at the light. This is called Kealakehe Parkway on the mountain side of the harbor and is 2.2 miles north of the Kailua-Kona Junction. After .3 of a mile toward the ocean, you will come to the harbor, where you should turn right. Drive through the harbor parking area, pass the restrooms, and continue to drive as far straight (west) as possible before parking. Ignore public access signs that will only make your hike longer.

From the end of the parking area, walk about 100 yards toward the water, then follow a sandy path that angles right for another 200 yards until you come to a T. At the T, turn left and you'll see the little sandy bay near the canoe shelter. Entry is from the far left because there's a bit more clearance on the left side. Snorkel wherever there is enough space. This isn't a good site for the claustrophobic. Fortunately, it tends to be very calm.

Honokohau Harbor (south)

This tiny cove, called 'Alula Cove, is close to the harbor, but feels secluded. It's shape offers protection from swells and it's just deep enough for good snorkeling. Although there are no facilities here, restrooms and showers are located back in the harbor parking lot.

Entry is easy from the sandy beach. Beginners can stay near shore, while experienced snorkelers will enjoy swimming beyond the point to the left and roaming out in the deeper water. The area is calm enough that it's a popular excursion destination. This is a nice safe spot to come with children since the beach is so gentle. Great spot for beginning snorkelers because it's calm and the swim is short, but beginners may prefer high tide for the best clearance.

GETTING THERE   From Highway 19, take the Honokohau Harbor entrance. This is 2.2 miles north of the Kailua-Kona Junction. Follow the road to the left side of the harbor (see map, page 83). Continue past the restrooms and shower and park at the far western end where the road becomes sand. Park here on the sand and you'll see the pretty cove to your left. This spot is about .9 of a mile from the highway. Park and hike about 150 yards over lava and rocks to the small sandy beach. Wearing shoes is a good idea. Snorkel straight out and around the point to the left when conditions are calm enough.

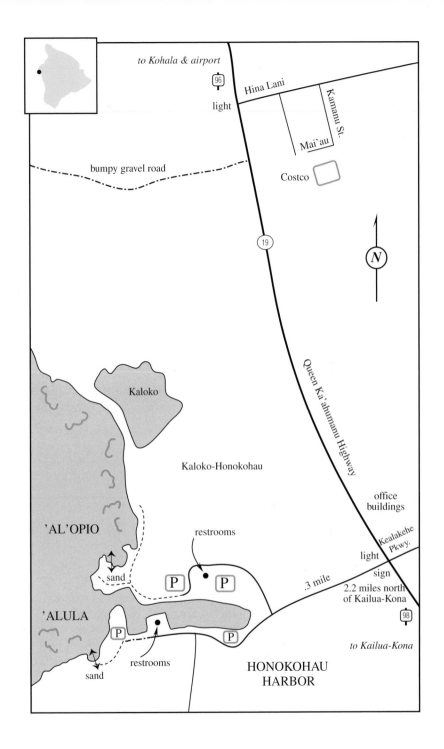

to Kohala & airport

96

Hina Lani

light

Kamanu St.

Mai'au

Costco

bumpy gravel road

N

19

Queen Ka'ahumanu Highway

Kaloko

Kaloko-Honokohau

'AL'OPIO

restrooms

office
buildings

Kealakehe Pkwy.

sand

light

P   P

sign

.3 mile

2.2 miles north
of Kailua-Kona

'ALULA

98

P

P

to Kailua-Kona

restrooms

HONOKOHAU
HARBOR

sand

Old Kona Airport Beach (Pawai Bay)

Even in very small swells, this entry can be quite difficult because the rocks are slippery and there are lots of spiny sea urchins. In fact, we once helped a tourist remove spines from her foot here. While the sea urchins move around, they tend to frequent just this sort of rocky, shallow bay.

There are plenty of fish, but there isn't much coral near shore. When the water is calm, you can snorkel to the right around the point and along a rocky ledge, which is more interesting. Many snorkel and dive boats come to the deeper area regularly. Snorkeling from shore requires calm seas so that you can venture further out for the best snorkeling. Snorkel as far to the right as comfortable. Currents here tend to flow to the left (south).

This is a nice picnic spot and a local hangout, which lends color, as long as the guys hanging out drinking beer don't make you nervous. And, if you always wanted to drive on an airport runway, here's your chance! Facilities include restrooms, showers, parking and picnic tables back on the ocean side of the runway.

GETTING THERE   Take the Kuakini Highway north from Palani Road (the main drag in Kailua-Kona). This intersection is more or less the center of town. Follow Kuakini north.

You'll pass playing fields on your left, jog a bit to the left, then the road eventually becomes an airport landing strip. Drive on the landing strip to the far end (at the north). Park here and walk out a short way to the end of the beach. It isn't far, but best to wear shoes. Little shade is available on the path. Facilities are located makai the runway.

Baby Beach

This small, but attractive beach is called Baby Beach because it's so well-protected and shallow. While it doesn't really provide snorkeling (well, a few fish) or swimming, we did want to mention the calm conditions in case you encounter rough water elsewhere. Baby Beach is not easy to find and has no facilities, but offers a nice spot to picnic and cool off. You'll find white sand, pretty small bays, 2 foot deep water, and a protecting natural lava "breakwater" that stops the waves completely. Sand level will vary with the season, with more in the summer. A perfect spot for small children.

GETTING THERE   From Highway 17 north of Kailua-Kona, take Makala Blvd. (at a light) toward the ocean. Turn left on Kuakini Highway and watch for the Kona Community Aquatic Center on your right (just north of Kaiwi Street). Park in back of the

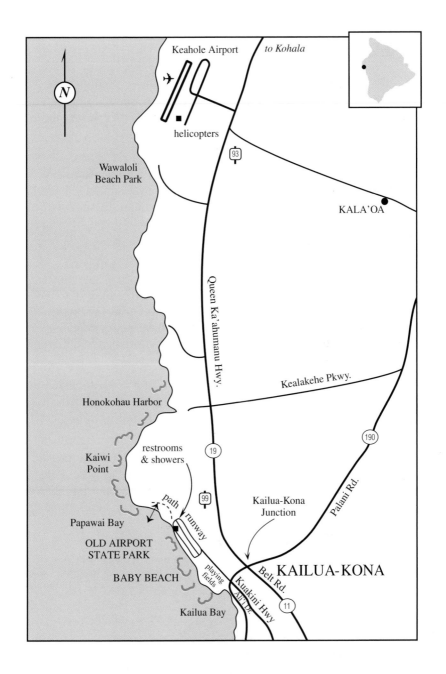

swim center, then walk through the gate in the chain-link fence, cross the soccer field (about 100 yards) angling left to another gate, where you will see public access signs. They will guide you down the steps, across the street, and into a 40-foot path to the little beach. From Kailua-Kona, just walk or drive north on Kuakini Highway, watching for the swim center on your left.

Kona/Keauhou area

This five-mile long area within North Kona district contains most of the condos and many of the hotels on the Big Island. Since so many tourists stay between the towns of Kailua-Kona and Keauhou, we've included it as a separate area.

Most of the coast here is rugged a'a lava, but there are scattered patches of sand beaches. These beaches usually have considerably more sand in the summer. Winter storms take away sand and calm summer seas return it. Fresh water springs pour into the shallow bays along this coast, so you may be surprised to find cooler water in the most protected bays.

When swells are low enough, there is usually some snorkeling within a mile or so of most hotels. All these sites are usable only in calm swell conditions. Only Kahalu'u Beach and Keauhou Bay have reliably calm water for beginners. Both beaches bordering the Kailua-Kona pier are the next most likely to have safe conditions. In-between beaches, like La'aloa and Pahoehoe, are better suited to more experienced snorkelers.

Kahalu'u Beach offers lots of BIG fish and comfortably shallow water. It's practically an aquarium full of large, magnificent fish that will let you come very close. Don't look for pristine coral here. Years of traffic have taken a heavy toll on the coral.

Keauhou Bay tends to be very murky near the entrance, but has an excellent reef with good visibility further out in the bay, where the water is about twenty-feet deep. Few boats use the harbor and they always stay in the channel at the center, so snorkeling here can be quite safe when seas are fairly calm.

oval butterflyfish

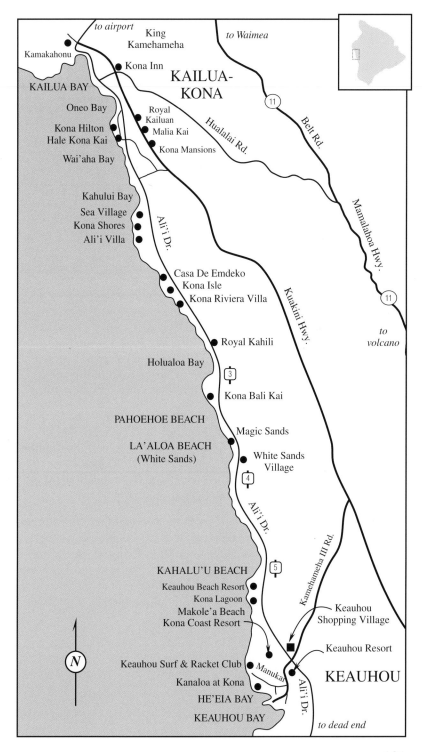

to airport

King
Kamehameha

to Waimea

Kamakahonu

Kona Inn

**KAILUA-
KONA**

KAILUA BAY

Oneo Bay

Royal
Kailuan

Malia Kai

11

Hualalai Rd.

Belt Rd.

Kona Hilton
Hale Kona Kai

Kona Mansions

Wai'aha Bay

Kahului Bay
Sea Village
Kona Shores
Ali'i Villa

Ali'i Dr.

Mamalahoa Hwy.

Casa De Emdeko
Kona Isle
Kona Riviera Villa

11

to
volcano

Royal Kahili

Kuakini Hwy.

Holualoa Bay

3

Kona Bali Kai

PAHOEHOE BEACH

Magic Sands

LA'ALOA BEACH
(White Sands)

White Sands
Village

4

Ali'i Dr.

KAHALU'U BEACH

5

Keauhou Beach Resort
Kona Lagoon
Makole'a Beach
Kona Coast Resort

Keauhou
Shopping Village

Kamehameha III Rd.

Keauhou Resort

N

Keauhou Surf & Racket Club

Manukai

KEAUHOU

Kanaloa at Kona

Ali'i Dr.

HE'EIA BAY

KEAUHOU BAY

to dead end

Kamakahonu Beach

This little beach offers good and easy snorkeling. Parking is difficult to find here in the center of Kailua-Kona, but you might give it a try if you're staying nearby. Entry is easy from the sand in the usually-calm bay. To snorkel, stay on your right (west) and swim along the lava rocks as far as seems safe.

GETTING THERE   Follow directions for Kailua-Kona Pier (below). The hard part is finding a parking space—either in the pay lots or in one of the few free spaces on the streets. Walk toward the Kamehameha Hotel (often called King Kam). This narrow bay is found to the west of the pier, where you can enter the water without worrying about boat traffic. Snorkel to the right, but watch for rough water, and don't head into strong or breaking swell. Snorkeling is surprisingly good considering the crowded location. Stay near the coast to avoid boat traffic.

Kailua-Kona Pier

Kailua-Kona is where the action is on the Big Island—you'll go there to shop, to eat, or to hang out. This bustling town has grown up, or perhaps sprawled around a core of historical buildings that may merit a visit during those odd hours that you're not snorkeling.

The Kailua harbor offers great protection and very easy entrance as long as you don't mind sharing the water with large boats. There's actually good snorkeling if you follow the pier, then continue up the coast to the northwest. The easiest entry is via the Kamakahonu Beach (see above), just west of the pier. If small waves are breaking onto the coast, it's still easy to stay beyond them.

The harbor area is often calm—something to remember on a stormy day. Use fins anyway because you may want to swim quite a long ways along the coast. This happens to be the site of the start of the Ironman Triathlon competition, so there's no chance to snorkel when this popular event takes place. Watch carefully for boat traffic as you snorkel beyond the inner bay to your right along the lava shoreline.

GETTING THERE   Take Highway 19 south past the airport, till you see the signs at Palani Road for Kailua-Kona (see map, page 101). Turn west at the Kailua-Kona Junction to drop down into town. As you pass the King Kamehameha Hotel on the right, and the road takes a 90° turn left, the pier is straight ahead. At this corner, Palani Road becomes Ali'i Drive.

Parking in town can look impossible, but if you keep trying, you can usually find space in one of the lots up the hill from Ali'i Drive.

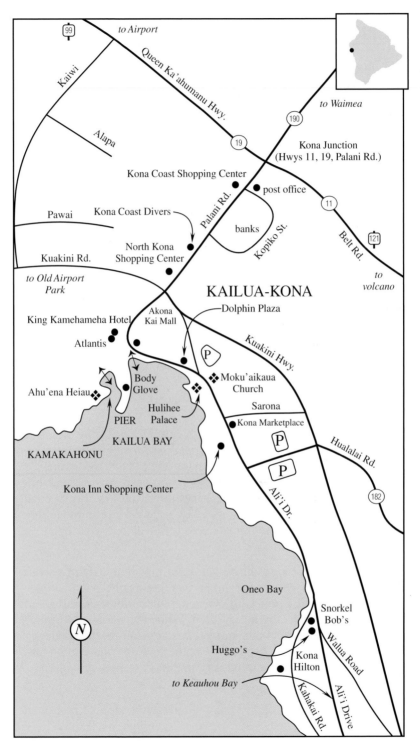

to Airport

Kaiwi

99

Queen Ka'ahumanu Hwy.

Alapa

19

190

to Waimea

Kona Junction
(Hwys 11, 19, Palani Rd.)

Kona Coast Shopping Center

post office

Pawai

Kona Coast Divers

banks

Palani Rd.

Kopiko St.

11

121

Belt Rd.

to
volcano

Kuakini Rd.

North Kona
Shopping Center

to Old Airport
Park

KAILUA-KONA

Akona
Kai Mall

Dolphin Plaza

Kuakini Hwy.

King Kamehameha Hotel

Atlantis

P

Moku'aikaua
Church

Body
Glove

Ahu'ena Heiau

Sarona

Hulihee
Palace

Kona Marketplace

PIER

P

KAILUA BAY

Hualalai Rd.

KAMAKAHONU

P

182

Kona Inn Shopping Center

Ali'i Dr.

N

Oneo Bay

Snorkel
Bob's

Huggo's

Kona
Hilton

Walua Road

to Keauhou Bay

Kahakai Rd.

Ali'i Drive

103

Pahoehoe Beach Park

This long, narrow park, located on the beach side (makai) of Ali'i Drive south of Kailua-Kona, takes its name from the smooth pahoehoe lava. It's a good picnic spot with grass and lots of shade. Portapotties are located at the northern end.

Since there is more lava than sand, this isn't the safest entry for snorkeling—especially when waves are kicking up. Early mornings are the best time to catch calm conditions. Even then, Kahalu'u, just a couple of miles south, is usually a better choice. When seas are very calm, you can snorkel all along this lava shoreline. Just be sure you aren't caught between a wave and that hard lava. Do stick with the sand entrance. While mornings are best, the sea sometimes gets very calm again in the late afternoon.

GETTING THERE   From Kailua-Kona, go south on Ali'i Drive about three miles watching closely on your right (see map, page 101). There's a sign near the center of the park and parking on the beach side of the road. If conditions aren't calm enough, continue south on Ali'i Drive. The next beach (White Sands) is usually calmer, while Kahalu'u Beach offers the very best protection from swells

La'aloa Beach Park (White Sands)

La'aloa Beach (also known as White Sands, Disappearing Sands or Magic Sands Beach) is easy to find and convenient (see map, page 101). It's a short walk from many condos and provides a convenient spot here for swimming or snorkeling if you don't have a car. While people do snorkel and swim straight off the lava rocks, this can lead to real trouble if the surf picks up. Leave such risky business to the most experienced local swimmers, and try La'aloa as your entry point instead.

As these various names indicate, sand can vanish quickly in a winter storm. It can all disappear overnight, just like magic. When ample sand is in place, it's a pretty little beach, popular for swimming and body-surfing—especially for children. When the waves aren't too high, swim beyond them and snorkel this area toward the south along the rocks or north around the point. You don't have to go far to avoid the crowds. We've seen very few snorkelers here—often just a couple.

Facilities include a small parking area, lifeguard, shower, restrooms and picnic tables. When White Sands is too rough, head south to

104

Kahalu'u. Mornings and low tide are your best bet at White Sands. Often it's more of a body-surfing beach, but is pretty and worth a try. Snorkeling is best to the right along the lava shoreline, but currents and breaking waves can be a problem, so watch carefully and consult the lifeguard.

GETTING THERE   Take Ali'i Drive south from Kailua-Kona about four miles from the King Kamehameha Hotel, where Palani Road becomes Ali'i Drive. You'll pass lots of condos and this is the first beach with facilities that you'll see. It's right along the road (see map, page 101).

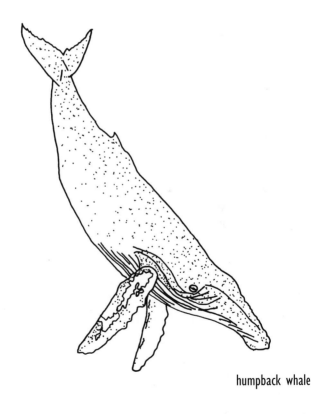

humpback whale

Kahalu'u Beach Park

Kahalu'u Beach (sometimes called Children's Beach) is adjacent to the road, and clearly marked. It's small, but has ample parking, white sand, showers, restrooms, a covered picnic area, lifeguard and a protecting breakwater, creating a walk-in aquarium.

This is a good site for beginners because it's calm, has fairly easy entry (if you don't mind snorkeling around lots of legs) and an abundance of unusually large, gorgeous fish. It's all fairly shallow and the fish are often fed, so they are practically tame and can be seen up-close. This makes for excellent photo opportunities.

Please do not feed the fish because this disrupts the natural order, and leads to ultimately lower fish numbers, as well as aggressive fish behavior. We're seeing greater than normal numbers of black durgons (somewhat of a weed fish) here—the more aggressive ones that crowd out other varieties of fish. Large turtles hang out here and seem able to completely ignore the tourists.

The shallowness makes beginners comfortable, although crowds of snorkelers in a narrow, shallow entry can be unnerving—even dangerous. Come early or late, avoid weekends, or swim out beyond the crowds and this is a reliable snorkeler's delight. Just get off the plane, grab swimsuit, mask, snorkel and fins (even if it's late afternoon) and head for Kahalu'u. It's the quickest way to start enjoying your vacation.

Some of you will be put off by the crowds, the fed fish, or the ruined reef tops from too much reef walking. Do your part by not standing on coral, or even touching it. There is no question that this is not a wilderness experience. Despite that, if you pick your time right, and you swim out a bit, the superb collection of large specimens of spectacular fish still makes this spot worth a visit.

Besides the resident turtles, we have seen parrotfish, Picasso triggerfish, groups of scrawled filefish, Moorish idols, raccoon butterflyfish, Achilles tang, threadfin butterflyfish, blue-stripe snapper, ornate butterflyfish, pinktail triggerfish, yellow tang, trumpetfish, spotted trunkfish—well, you get the idea. We even spotted a rarely-seen tiny dragon wrasse flip-flopping along the sand, doing its best to look like a piece of seaweed.

A word of caution though: when the surf kicks up, even if it's stopped by the breakwater, there's still plenty of current caused by the water coming in over the partial breakwater. The current has

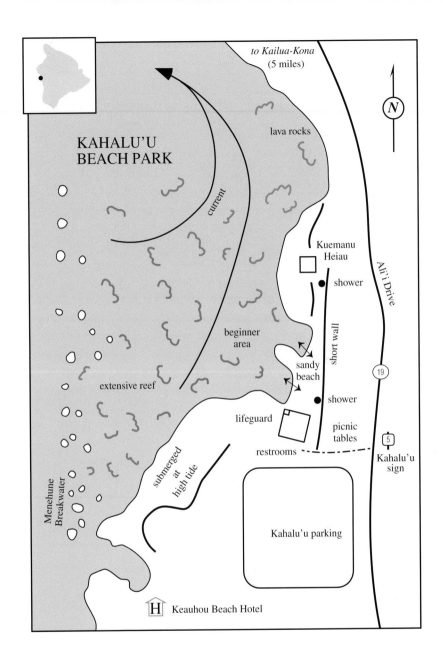

to Kailua-Kona
(5 miles)

N

KAHALU'U
BEACH PARK

lava rocks

current

Kuemanu
Heiau

shower

Ali'i Drive

beginner
area

short wall

sandy
beach

extensive reef

shower

19

lifeguard

picnic
tables

submerged at high tide

restrooms

5

Kahalu'u
sign

Menehune Breakwater

Kahalu'u parking

H Keauhou Beach Hotel

107

a tendency to sweep north and then out, so stay closer to shore during storms and always wear fins.

If caught by the current, don't panic. It's much better to float out beyond the breaking waves and wait for help than to try to swim back across rocks or lava. At Kahalu'u Beach Park, at least, someone is likely to see you. Keep in mind that rip currents usually don't take you more than a few hundred feet (see Rip Currents, page 28 for more details). It's just a matter of all that water pouring in and needing somewhere to get out.

Early mornings and late afternoons are best to avoid the crowds. High tide provides a wider area with comfortable clearance. Low tide is OK, but you won't be able to explore all the nice, shallow corners along the lava to the left.

And, once again, please don't stand on the living reef no matter how tempting. If you must stand up, pick a patch of bare sand so you do no harm.

GETTING THERE   Take Ali'i Drive south from Kailua-Kona (see area map, page 101) to the 5 mile mark (about a mile south of La'aloa Beach) and you can't miss this small park. See map, page 107 for the details of entry and where to snorkel. It's located immediately to the north of the Keauhou Resort. For the best fish viewing, swim just beyond the crowds.

pinktail triggerfish

Disposable Underwater Cameras

Cheap, widely available, even stocked on some excursions, and fun to use. Keep your expectations realistic and you won't end up disappointed. You simply won't get pictures like you see in National Geographic. The professionals who get all those great shots use camera setups worth $10,000 and more. They also have assistants underwater to hold the lights and spare cameras. Their books start to look like bargains compared with trying to get these pictures by yourself. Check out the great selection of marine life books in Big Island bookstores.

Still, it's fun to try for that cute shot of your sweetie in a bikini, clowning with the fish. If you're lucky, you'll actually have identifiable fish in a few shots. The cameras won't focus closer than about four feet, so the fish will look much smaller than you remember them. These cameras work best when it's sunny with good visibility and the subject fish as close as the camera allows.

They do work OK above the water too, so make a great knock-around camera to haul around wet or dry without paranoia about theft, saltwater or damage. Try a picture of the beautiful mountains of North Kohala as you float in the waters of Kauna'oa Bay.

longnose butterflyfish

Keauhou area

We've included a Keauhou map since the streets here are confusing and many of you will need to find Keauhou Harbor for excursions. Harbors are often the last place you'd want to snorkel, but this one is really quite good, with very little boat traffic. It's large enough for two snorkeling trips (one for each side) and usually calm with easy access—a real plus if you're looking for a site close to Kailua-Kona and don't mind the deeper water. The harbor is also a great place to begin a kayaking trip.

raccoon butterflyfish

He'eia Bay

He'eia Bay is also known as Walker Bay. You can snorkel here without worrying about boats or crowds. Entry is slightly tricky, since it's fairly shallow and more rocky than sandy. The bay is long and narrow, so it can be quite protected when the wave angle is favorable. Snorkel anywhere within the bay or beyond to nearby Keauhou Bay when weather permits. No facilities are available at He'eia Bay. There's a sand/gravel beach, but it's not the sandiest or the prettiest. Some seasons, the beach is all rock. This is an OK place for snorkeling, but not as good for swimming due to the rocks.

Narrow He'eia Bay is located just north of Keauhou Bay (an easy walk). It's tucked into a small residential area south of the Kanaloa development. There is public access from Manukai Street, although the path is somewhat hidden and overgrown.

GETTING THERE   If you happen to be staying near Kanaloa at Kona, He'eia Bay is just a short walk south. If you're driving, take King Kamehameha III Road from Highway 19 down the hill past Ali'i Drive, and turn right on Manukai Road. Watch on the left for a small street, then the path (see map, page 111).

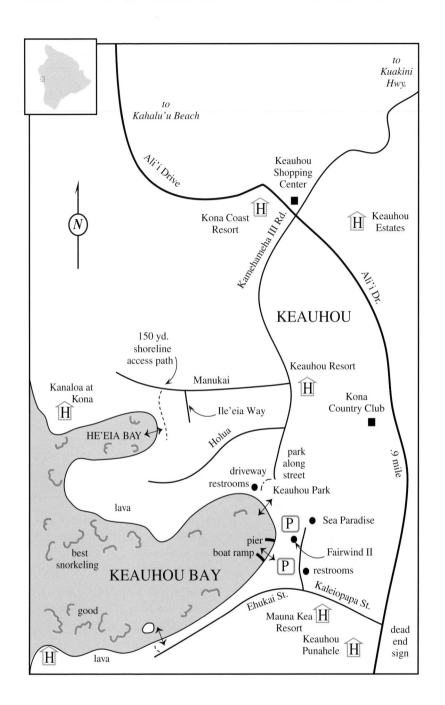

to
Kuakini
Hwy.

to
Kahalu'u Beach

Ali'i Drive

Keauhou
Shopping
Center

N

Kona Coast
Resort

Kamehameha III Rd.

H Keauhou
Estates

Ali'i Dr.

KEAUHOU

150 yd.
shoreline
access path

Manukai

Keauhou Resort

H

Kona
Country Club

Kanaloa at
Kona

H

Ile'eia Way

HE'EIA BAY

Holua

park
along
street

.9 mile

driveway
restrooms

Keauhou Park

lava

P

Sea Paradise

pier
boat ramp

P

Fairwind II

restrooms

best
snorkeling

KEAUHOU BAY

Kaleiopapa St.

good

Ehukai St.

Mauna Kea H
Resort

dead
end
sign

Keauhou H
Punahele

H

lava

Keauhou Bay

The Fair Wind and Sea Paradise offices are both located at Keauhou Harbor. The Fair Wind office is to the left of the pier, and the Sea Paradise office is on the right.

If you don't mind some boat traffic (although it's not frequent), this is an excellent place to snorkel and swim. There's a small park with a bit of sand, so enter along here. Choose whichever side of the bay is calmest. There's plenty of reef here, but stay inside the ample harbor away from any offshore currents and surf when stormy. Winter can sometimes bring big waves crashing spectacularly against the points, but the harbor itself is usually calm.

On the left side of the bay, the best snorkeling is out toward the point. There's plenty of good coral and fish here, so give it a try. You will need to swim a ways for the best snorkeling and clear water. We have seen lots of turtles, colorful Christmas wrasses, schools of raccoon butterflyfish, Moorish idols, pink and blue coral, but most after a fairly long swim. To shorten the swim a bit, you can always enter from the pier or boat ramp instead of the park area. All provide easy entry into the usually calm bay. A path near the island on the south side will place you closest to the best snorkeling, but isn't always easy for entry.

The north side of Keauhou Bay is even better. Snorkel along the right side about as far as a line connecting the points, then head back to the middle of the bay (stopping before the boat channel). The first time we headed way out here, we were surprised at how much the visibility and quality of coral improved as we left the inner harbor. There is plenty of room to explore when swells aren't too high. Visibility is much better out here than you might expect when you enter the water, where murky water cuts into your snorkeling enjoyment.

Keauhou Bay offers an excellent kayaking entry from either the park to the north or the boat ramp to the south. When seas are calm, you can kayak out of the bay and along the Kona coast in either direction–stopping to snorkel off the lava coast.

Manta rays like to gather at night in the 20'-deep water off the southern point, where the hotel used to shine bright lights to attract them. The hotel is closed now, but may do the same in the future. If so, it's possible to swim out here on a very calm night. The major hazard here is from dive boats, so you would need strong lights to be easily seen.

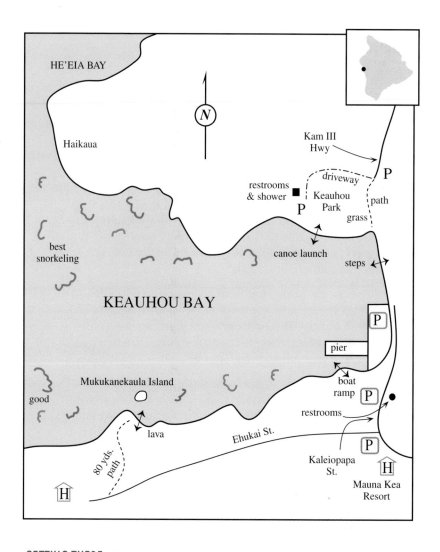

HE'EIA BAY

Haikaua

N

Kam III Hwy

P

restrooms & shower

driveway

Keauhou Park

P

path

grass

best snorkeling

canoe launch

steps

KEAUHOU BAY

P

pier

good

Mukukanekaula Island

boat ramp

P

lava

restrooms

P

80 yds. path

Ehukai St.

Kaleiopapa St.

H

Mauna Kea Resort

H

GETTING THERE For the easiest route to snorkeling, take the King Kamehameha III (called "Kam III") Highway exit from Highway 11 in Keauhou. Follow Kam III to the very end and park along the side of the road. Follow the short path or driveway to the park and facilities (see area map, page 111).

To drive to the harbor from the corner of Ali'i Drive and Kamehameha III Road, go .9 mile south on Ali'i Drive. Turn right on Kaleiopapa Street at the "dead end" sign. Drive on to the "Keauhou Pier" sign. Park outside the tiny congested pier parking lot if you don't want to get stuck in a mini traffic jam. It's a short walk from the bigger parking lot. There is another lot for Fair Wind and Sea Paradise customers just up the street.

We review boat trips departing from Keauhou Harbor in the water excursion section beginning on page 152.

South Kona area

The Big Island takes on a greener, cooler look as you head south of Keauhou to the South Kona district. These steeper hills of South Kona are ideal for growing coffee, macadamia nuts, and tropical flowers. The bays are large and offer excellent snorkeling in beautiful settings.

Although there are no big hotels as we write, two huge and controversial luxury golf, homesite and condo developments are under construction just north of Kealakekua Bay. A third development that would reach close to the Monument appears to have been blocked, due to strong community opposition. Runoff from the golf courses and streets could gradually damage extraordinary and pristine Kealakeakua Bay.

Two bays in South Kona offer perhaps the best snorkeling in all the major Hawai'ian islands. Kealakekua Bay and Honaunau Bay are both tops on our list of snorkeling sites. They are large, usually calm, and have extensive reefs for exploration. Be sure to try both—unless you get very unlucky with the weather.

The Captain Cook monument in Kealakekua Bay is nearly always calm, but difficult to reach unless you take an excursion from Keauhou or kayak across the mile-wide bay. Strong swimmers can cross the bay, while strong hikers can make it down from the highway. Snorkeling near the monument in about ten feet of water is delightful—especially with the deep indigo of the bay right nearby. It's a chance to see plenty of reef fish near shore and pelagic creatures beyond the edge of the reef.

Increasingly-popular Honaunau Bay is easier to reach, with an entry from the smooth lava. You can also walk through the historical park and enter via a protected little bay where canoes were launched. This bay has reef throughout with varied depths, canyons and arches. Explore any direction within the protected bay to view a large variety of sea life. Beginners can stay near shore where the water is about ten feet deep.

Pu'uhonua O Honaunau National Historical Park (Place of Refuge) is an enchanting park, which shouldn't be missed with or without a snorkeling break.

Ke'ei, Ho'okina and Miloli'i Bays (all further south) also offer good snorkeling, but are considerably less protected and out of the way. They are more exposed to swells across shallow reefs, so they should only be attempted by experienced snorkelers.

114

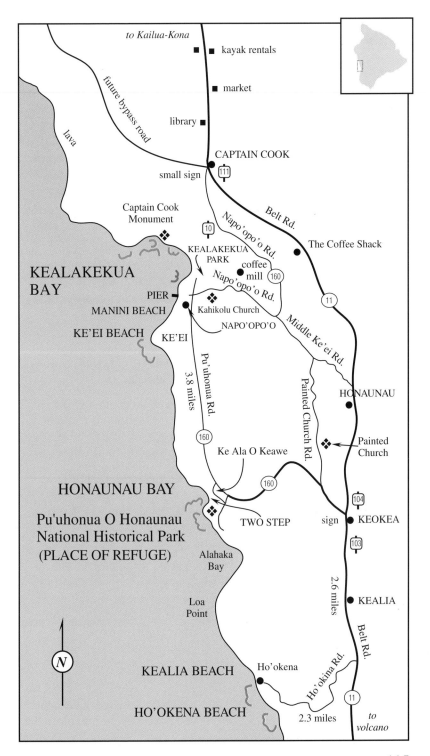

to Kailua-Kona

kayak rentals

market

library

CAPTAIN COOK
111

small sign

Belt Rd.

The Coffee Shack

future bypass road

lava

Captain Cook
Monument

10

Napo'opo'o Rd.

KEALAKEKUA
PARK

coffee
mill
160

Napo'opo'o Rd.

11

KEALAKEKUA
BAY

PIER

MANINI BEACH

KE'EI BEACH

KE'EI

Kahikolu Church

NAPO'OPO'O

Middle Ke'ei Rd.

Pu'uhonua Rd.

3.8 miles

160

Ke Ala O Keawe

HONAUNAU BAY

Pu'uhonua O Honaunau
National Historical Park
(PLACE OF REFUGE)

Painted Church Rd.

HONAUNAU

Painted
Church

160

104

TWO STEP

sign

KEOKEA

103

Alahaka
Bay

Loa
Point

2.6 miles

KEALIA

Belt Rd.

N

KEALIA BEACH

Ho'okena

HO'OKENA BEACH

Ho'okena Rd.

2.3 miles

11

to
volcano

Kealakekua Bay (Captain Cook Monument)

Beautiful Kealakekua Bay is about one mile wide, extending from the Captain Cook Monument on the north, to the former fishing community of Napo'opo'o in the south. It's usually quite calm and offers some of the best snorkeling in the Hawai'ian islands.

The bay tends to be unusually calm even in winter. With fins it's possible to swim the one mile across the bay (even less if you walk to the far end of the beach). To swim here, you'll need to cross the deep center of the bay or follow the cliffs from Napo'opo'o. This is a long swim, so you need to either be in good shape or allow plenty of time to rest along the way. Fins are essential and a wet suit makes it easier to stay as long as you like without getting chilled.

The middle of the bay is deep, without coral, but often has as many as 200 spinner dolphins playing around in small groups, or pods. It's quite a thrill to watch them swim under you and jump out of the water—sometimes spinning in the air!

The best snorkeling in Kealakekua Bay is found in the clear waters near the Captain Cook Monument, where you'll find coral, eels, turkeyfish, and an endless variety of colorful fish.

Very late afternoon might not be the best time to try this swim. The sea is often rougher then, and sharks are reputed to come in to feed as night approaches. We've only seen baby sharks here, and even then very rarely, though we often snorkel until sundown.

It's also possible to see this area by kayak, which can be rented in several shops up along the highway. If you do rent a kayak, make sure to enter the water from the pier area, rather than trying rough spots where you risk turning over on the lava. The shore west of the monument is a perfect spot to bring a picnic.

Whether you get here by a long swim, kayak, inflatable or with the popular Fair Wind excursion, you'll love the Captain Cook monument area with its 3-10' deep water near shore, dropping off into the deep indigo of the bay. To give you an idea of some of the sights: pufferfish, butterflyfish of all kinds (fourspot, raccoon, ornate, teardrop, milletseed, oval, reticulated), fantail filefish, Potter's angelfish, Triton's trumpet, eagle ray, turkeyfish, a variety of eels, triggerfish (Picasso, rectangular, lei), and much more.

The Captain Cook Monument, a 27'-high white obelisk marks the excellent snorkeling right in front. If you have a chance, explore the

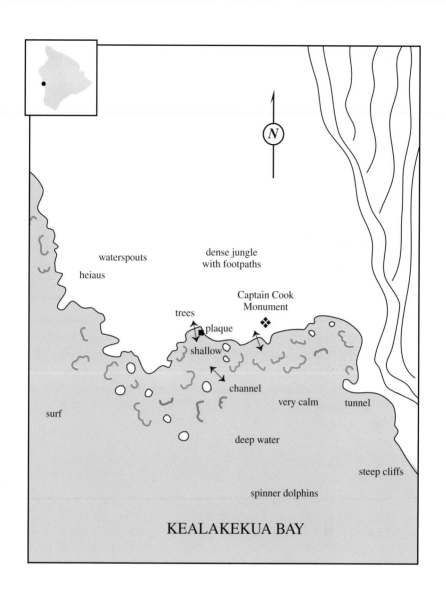

waterspouts

heiaus

dense jungle
with footpaths

Captain Cook
Monument

trees

plaque

shallow

channel

very calm

tunnel

surf

deep water

steep cliffs

spinner dolphins

KEALAKEKUA BAY

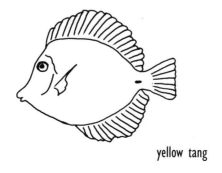

yellow tang

entire north side of Kealakekua Bay. The little kayak entrance to the west of the monument is also an excellent snorkeling area and you may even find the elusive bronze plaque, marking the spot where Captain Cook supposedly died. High tide will cover the plaque completely, but it's near shore in this little shallow cove.

GETTING THERE   Drive south on Highway 11 to almost the 111 mile marker (see area map, page 115). Watch for a Y with a small sign at Napo'opo'o Road. Head right, down the steep hill.

Some books suggest hiking to the monument from here—a locked gate blocks vehicles from the rugged, steep road. It's about a 1,500' drop to the water, the road is rough, indirect and unmarked, and there's no water available, so think long and hard before trying this. We talked to one couple who desperately tried to buy a ride up from the bottom with maintenance workers with no success. It made for a very bad first date.

It's a long, winding drive down the road to Napo'opo'o, but it's well worth it, as you wind through some strikingly beautiful greenery and flowers. At the bottom of the hill you drive directly ahead into the parking lot. To be a few hundred yards closer, it's also OK to turn right and park where the road ends, offering a nice view of the bay.

To the right of Kealakekua Park, you can see a rocky beach where entry to the water is quite easy. Reef shoes are needed because the beach has more pebbles and rocks than sand. It's possible to enter right at the end of the road, or walk to the far end and enter a bit closer to the monument. It just depends on whether you'd rather walk or swim. Enter from either the pier or this "beach" to swim across the bay to the monument area.

Just two boats have permission to anchor within the bay. Taking a comfortable boat that shades and feeds you is certainly a much easier way to get to the monument. In this particular case, we highly recommend the Fairwind II (see review, page 152).

The water tends to be very calm here, even when rough elsewhere. Since the snorkeling is so superb, it's great to save your time and energy for this incredible spot, where two hours pass in a flash. If you're serious about snorkeling or even willing to try it once, don't even think about missing this opportunity. Try to spot some of the beautiful Potter's angelfish in the shallow areas near shore, or look sharp for an octopus.

Zodiac trips also stop at several spots around the bay; however, they tend to stay just a short time in each location. This spot really merits several hours. The Fair WInd II seems to spend just about the right amount of time.

spotted boxfish

118

Discounts

Discounts are available for many excursions. If you're so inclined, a little work and the right questions can save you a fair chunk of change. Begin by picking up one of the numerous free promotional magazines such as Big Island Gold. These are readily available at the airport, hotels and shops. They usually include special offers, coupons and other deals to attract new customers.

Calling an excursion office and asking if there are any special offers can sometimes pay off, especially when tourism is slower. Summer and holidays the ships fill more quickly, but there is still plenty of competition in Hawai'i, so it's always worth a try.

Excursions often charge less for children and nothing for toddlers. Each has its own definition of child and adult. Don't hesitate to ask about senior discounts, repeat customer discounts, and kama'aina rate (only available if you live in the islands and can prove it by showing your driver's license). Sometimes discounts are provided to AAA members.

For discounts ranging from 10-20%, try Activity Warehouse: (800) 201-3999   web site: travelhawaii.com   They also offer a free aloha breakfast early in your trip, in exchange for sitting through their pitch.

For good deals, it helps to have a flexible schedule and be able to go at the last minute.

For a free trip or 2 for 1 deal, sign up for a timeshare offer. You will have to sit through an hour or two of sales talk in exchange for your bargain trip. Do not underestimate their sales ability!

When you do book tickets ahead of time and charge them to your credit card, remember that as long as the ship goes out, with or without you, you will be charged for the trip. The fine print usually requires you to cancel at least 24 hours ahead. You may wake up to weather that doesn't suit you only to find that the ship sailed anyway, and you will get to pay as agreed. Also, your destination isn't guaranteed. You might have your heart set on the reef at Puako, only to find the ship change to Pawai due to rough weather at Puako. This does not entitle you to cancel. Keep in mind they sometimes must make changes for safety reasons, so go with the flow and trust your captain.

Kealakekua Bay Park

This is a small park at the north end of the road when you drive down the hill to Napo'opo'o. While the beach here is more like pebbles than sand, it's often calm enough for swimming and has good snorkeling to the left and along the lava coast. Not as great as across the bay, but certainly worth checking out. If there are waves, stay beyond them for better visibility as well as safety. You'll find fairly large scattered coral heads in about fifteen feet of water from the "beach" as far as the pier. Snorkeling is best to the left of the beach and extends out to about fifty yards from shore.

GETTING THERE Drive south on Highway 11 to just before 111 mile marker and watch for a Y with a small sign at Napo'opo'o Rd. (see map, page 115). Head right, down the hill. Drive all the way down the hill through the lush jungle scenery. At the bottom, take a right turn and park at the end of the street—about a half block away. You'll see the park toward your right and the beach straight ahead. In winter the waves may be too rough, but conditions change often. When calm enough, snorkel from the beach to the left staying along the coast. The best snorkeling is between the pier and the "beach." For a VERY long snorkel, head to the right all the way to the Captain Cook Monument. Only very strong swimmers should attempt this.

Napo'opo'o Pier

The pier offers parking and the easiest entry when the ocean is a bit rough at the beach. The pier may look too high for easy entry when tide is low, but there's a secret. Look at the spot marked on our map for the steps that can't be seen well from above. If in doubt, the local kids can also show you the steps.

Snorkeling is best to the right within about fifty yards of the lava shoreline. You can also head to the left to explore a large area with scattered coral heads. Sometimes the fish will be plentiful all over this area, while other days are a bit disappointing. Allow plenty of clearance if waves are crashing on the lava. This pier is also the easiest spot to launch a kayak for a memorable trip to the Captain Cook Monument.

GETTING THERE Drive south on Highway 11 to almost the 111 mile marker, watching for a Y with a small sign at Napo'opo'o Road (see area map, page 115). Head right, down the hill. Wind all the way down the hill through the lush jungle scenery and you will eventually hit the Napo'opo'o Pier parking lot—straight in front of you. Park in the dirt lot and walk out on the old pier. The steps and kayak launching area are located on the left side of the far end of the pier, where it is usually completely calm.

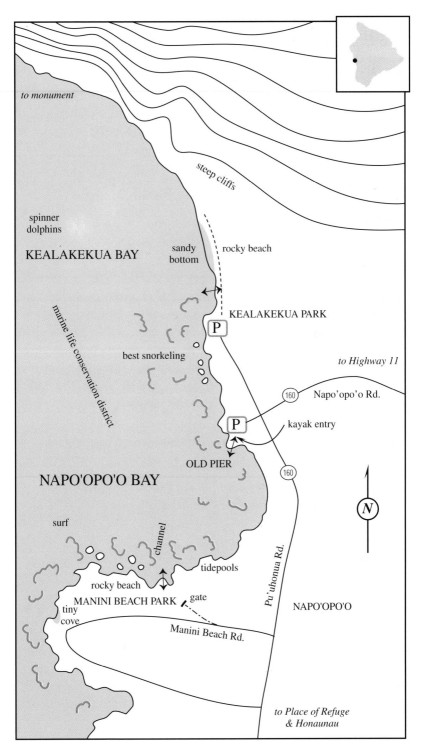

to monument

spinner
dolphins

KEALAKEKUA BAY

marine life conservation district

sandy
bottom

rocky beach

steep cliffs

KEALAKEKUA PARK

P

best snorkeling

to Highway 11

160 Napo'opo'o Rd.

P

kayak entry

OLD PIER

160

NAPO'OPO'O BAY

N

surf

channel

tidepools

rocky beach

MANINI BEACH PARK

gate

tiny
cove

Pu'uhonua Rd.

NAPO'OPO'O

Manini Beach Rd.

to Place of Refuge
& Honaunau

121

Manini Beach Park

This little public park has no facilities except picnic tables. The "sand" is really chunks of black lava and white coral. It's pretty, and there's an easy entry point if you're wearing booties. Otherwise, it's awfully sharp on the feet. The only snorkeling entry point is through a little channel at the far right side (east end) of the beach. Angle to the right and snorkel out where there is enough clearance. Continue to the right because the left is usually rougher.

High tide is a real plus here for entry, because there's precious little clearance during low tide. Once out in the bay, there's plenty of space for comfort as you swim above the coral heads. Fish can be abundant or disappointing, depending on the day you snorkel, so that will affect your opinion of this bay.

The rest of this long beach (to the west) is too rocky for good swimming or snorkeling. Depending on the season and wave conditions, you will find some excellent tidepools just to the east of the park— some about hot tub size.

Manini Park is a beautiful, peaceful spot for a picnic with views of the Captain Cook Monument area across the bay. Locals like to picnic here, so be respectful of their space. Watch for the 200-250 spinner dolphins who love to cavort in Kealakekua Bay.

GETTING THERE   Drive south on Highway 11 to almost the 111 mile marker (see area map, page 115), watching for a Y with a small sign at Napo'opo'o Road. Head right, down the hill. Wind all the way down the hill through the lush jungle scenery (see map, page 121). At the bottom of the hill, take a left turn. Then, the first right on Manini Beach Road. You'll pass a few houses before seeing the eastern corner of the park. Usually the entrance is chained. If so, just park along the street and walk the short way in. The snorkeling entry is near this entrance.

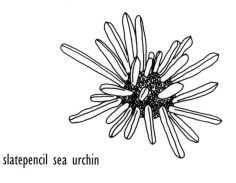

slatepencil sea urchin

Dive Boats

PADI and NAUI attempt to regulate the diving industry with strict rules, since there are serious risks involved. No one is allowed to dive without certification (a C card). Anyone who wants to dive without proper training is certainly a fool, and the shops who will take such rash people out are equally foolish.

We have seen excursions all over the world offering to take people down without proof of certification. This is not the mark of the highest level of safety consciousness. Keep in mind that other advice and services from such operators may be similarly casual. Always take extra care with any rental equipment.

When their business is slow, some take divers (or snorkelers) to sites they can't handle. On the better snorkeling excursions, they keep a close eye on all their charges, so it's like having a lifeguard along.

Tagging along with a dive boat, you may find yourself on the surface as a snorkeler in much rougher conditions than the divers 60 feet beneath you. You'll need to rely on a buddy since the crew is usually more focused on the divers. It's a good idea to ask in advance whether good snorkeling is possible at the particular dive site they are planning for that day.

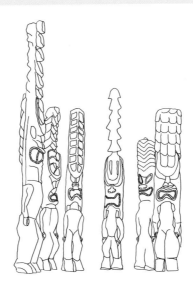

Ke'ei Beach

This well-hidden beach has excellent snorkeling when conditions are calm, but is often unsafe—especially in the winter. The coast is very rocky here and doesn't have the protection found in the nearby bays, so it isn't worth the drive unless you're certain swells are low. When calm, there's plenty of room to explore, with good coral, canyons, and arches. Just make sure you don't end up between a wave and some lava or coral. Ke'ei is for experienced snorkelers only due to its isolation and exposure to waves. With a rental car, you might prefer to avoid this very bumpy road.

GETTING THERE   Located between Kealakekua Bay and Honaunau Bay, access is from Pu'uhonua Road connecting these two bays (see area map, page 115). From the town of Napo'opo'o, take Pu'uhonua Road toward Place of Refuge (see map, page 125). Go about .5 of a mile from town, pass Keawaiki Road with its bunch of mailboxes, then take the next right toward the water. It's unmarked and very bumpy.

Follow this road across the bare lava field as it turns left in about .2 of a mile, then continue another .2 of a mile. The road gets worse and worse, so you might as well park about here. If the sea is calm enough, you can enter from the lava here. Or, you can brave more poor road for another .2 of a mile to some picnic tables and another lava entry. Going the last bit to the sandy beach is hard on the car. Drive very slow and avoid this road after heavy rain. Local people will appreciate you driving slow since their houses are quite near the street, and children may be playing in the area.

The coast at Ke'ei is quite rocky and mostly shallow, so we don't advise snorkeling unless conditions are extremely calm. Leave something noticable or bright when you enter in order to find your way back for exit. You'll need to weave your way around shallow areas to reach the more comfortable depth at the far edge of the reef.

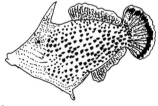

fantail filefish

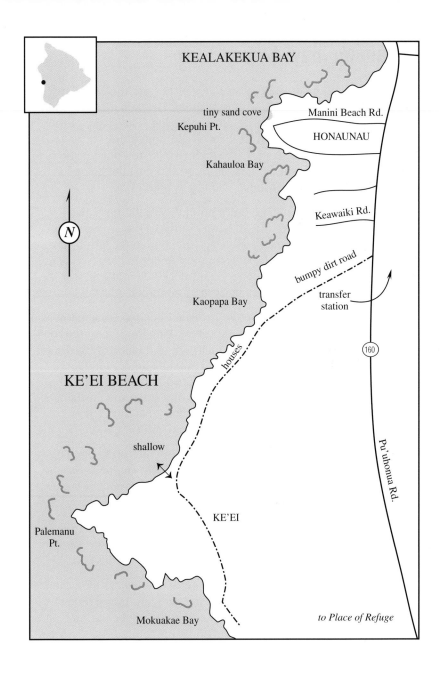

KEALAKEKUA BAY

tiny sand cove

Kepuhi Pt.

Manini Beach Rd.

HONAUNAU

Kahauloa Bay

Keawaiki Rd.

N

bumpy dirt road

Kaopapa Bay

transfer
station

160

houses

KE'EI BEACH

shallow

Pu'uhonua Rd.

Palemanu
Pt.

KE'EI

Mokuakae Bay

to Place of Refuge

Honaunau Bay (Two Step)

Located just a short walk north of Place of Refuge, this popular snorkeling site is one of the very best in the Hawai'ian islands. The whole bay offers exciting and varied snorkeling. The shape of the bay provides good protection from swells, although the exit onto lava can be a bit challenging even with small swells. You need enough experience to enter from the lava shore, so this isn't the place for timid first-time snorkelers unless the bay is really flat.

Two Step got it name from an entry point where there are two distinct bench-like ledges making entry and exit easier. We've marked the spot on our map (see page 127), but you're also likely to see local snorkelers and sun-bathers entering here unless you arrive quite early. This smooth pahoehoe lava offers easy walking, but the sun heats it enough to require shoes in the summer.

Two Step has become very popular, so you'll need to come early to be assured of parking in the limited spots along the side of the road. When all else fails, there's parking nearby in the Place of Refuge lot, although you'll need to pay the very reasonable admission fee ($5 per car at the moment, but good for a week). Portapotties are available along the road, while restrooms and water are available near the exhibits in Place of Refuge. You may also find private parking across the street from Two Step for only $2.

All of Honaunau Bay is full of coral, fish, canyons, arches and ranges from 5-50 feet deep. If you want to stay in shallower water (about 5-10'), just snorkel to the right closer to the lava. The deepest canyons are to the left and out a bit near the Place of Refuge.

If you're not comfortable exiting on lava or if swells pick up, the boat channel is always available. It's easy and safe, but very shallow at low tide. This is tucked between the lava entry and the park.

You're almost sure to see turtles here—especially where the water drops to 20 feet. And, of course, the usual wrasses, tangs, butterfly-fish, eels, and even some larger pelagic fish. We've seen schools of at least 50 nocturnal raccoon butterflyfish lazing around. We even got lucky once and saw two white-tipped reef sharks cruising the outer deeper area. We also spotted a couple of titan triggerfish, something we haven't seen elsewhere in Hawai'i. Take our word for it; you'll want to return to Two Step every time you visit the Big Island.

No facilities other than the portapotties, a couple of shaded picnic tables, boat ramp, and a handful of parking spaces intended

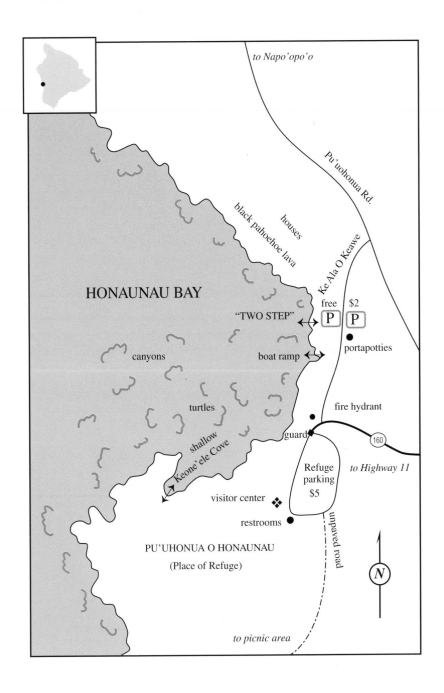

to Napo'opo'o

Pu'uohonua Rd.

black pahoehoe lava

houses

Ke Ala O Keawe

HONAUNAU BAY

"TWO STEP" ←→

free $2

P P

● portapotties

canyons

boat ramp ←→

turtles

fire hydrant

●

shallow
Keone'ele Cove

●

guard →

160

Refuge
parking
$5

to Highway 11

visitor center ❖

restrooms ●

unpaved road

PU'UHONUA O HONAUNAU

(Place of Refuge)

N

to picnic area

primarily for boat trailers. Just gorgeous views, a great adjacent historical site, and some of the island's best and most varied snorkeling, with easy entry and exit, make this a thoroughly outstanding snorkeling site.

Two Step is our personal favorite snorkeling site in all of the Hawai'ian islands. It lacks a sandy beach and seclusion, but offers a great variety of sea life as well as fairly reliable conditions year round.

GETTING THERE Drive south on Highway 11 from Kailua-Kona and turn right at the well-marked sign for Place of Refuge (Highway 160) at mile marker 104 (see area map, page 115). Follow this road down to the ocean and pass the entrance to Place of Refuge (see site map, page 125). About 50 feet past the entrance stay left along the ocean and you'll see Honaunau Bay with a boat ramp and some parking along the road. Park near the
portapotties and picnic tables if space is available. Walk an easy 100 feet across the smooth black lava (pahoehoe) and look for the best entry. Unless you arrive very early, you'll find a cluster of snorkelers or divers at this spot. Don't make the mistake of trying to get in or out too far to the right. Look for the bench-like ledge to sit on and put on your fins.

From Kealakekua Bay, you can take Pu'uhonua Road, a straight and narrow four-mile long road connecting the two bays. Stay makai (toward the ocean) at the Y and you'll come to Two Step.

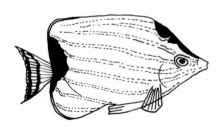

bluestripe butterflyfish

I Like to Watch

"For some reason, the barracuda don't seem scary, any more than the ray does. For some reason, none of this seems scary. Even the idea of maybe encountering a smallish s___k doesn't seem altogether bad.

It's beginning to dawn on me that all the fish and eels and crabs and shrimps and plankton who live and work down here are just too busy to be thinking about me.

I'm a traveller from another dimension, not really a part of their already event-filled world, not programmed one way or another—food or yikes—into their instinct circuits. They have important matters to attend to, and they don't care whether I watch or not. And so I watch."

—Dave Barry

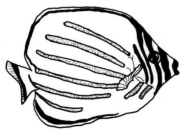

ornate butterflyfish

Pu'uhonua O Honaunau (Place of Refuge)

Pu'uhonua O Honaunau National Historical Park, called Place of Refuge by most tourists, offers excellent and varied snorkeling. There are three quite different sites that we highly recommend. Most tourists think they can't snorkel in the park, so they go right at the fire hydrant just before the parking lot, then park along the road and enter the water from there—where it's called Two Step. This gives access to all of Honaunau Bay. See page 126 for details.

From Two Step you can snorkel as far as you like to the left along the edge of the park passing boulders through 20-30' deep clear water where we have seen lots of large and small fish, more turtles, eels, interesting coral and great canyons.

It's even more fun to enter through the park. At the guard station, pay $5 per car for parking and use of all facilities, an excellent value since the permit is valid for a week. This is a fascinating and beautiful place that shouldn't be missed, so allow time to stroll around the grounds. The exhibits are interesting, and there's a well-marked trail. This is a religious site, and it does certainly have a serene and spiritual feeling. The information desk has an excellent brochure with map of the park and sells fish ID books as well as a large map of the Big Island.

Due to the historical character of the park, beach users and snorkelers are not allowed to leave anything on the grounds (including towels). Just suit up at your car and walk through the beautiful, shaded grounds to the right to the little shallow beach (actually a canoe entrance). You may catch some odd looks from other tourists who wonder why you're here carrying snorkel gear, but the park rangers at the front desk insist that it's perfectly OK. Swim out this old canoe channel and you're right in the middle of the best snorkeling. High tide is best if you like plenty of clearance for entry and exit. Several turtles frequent this shallow cove.

This isn't the best plan on a hot day if you don't wear booties, because the parking lot will be too hot for bare feet.

GETTING THERE   From Highway 11 (see area map, page 115), drive south about seven miles past the Kealakekua turnoff. Take Highway 160 toward the water (between markers 103 and 104). It's an excellent road and well-marked. Near the water you'll see a sign on the left to the parking lot.

Alternately, you can get from Napo'opo'o by taking the straight one-lane Pu'uhonua Road across the lava four miles south. It joins the highway near the entrance to the park.

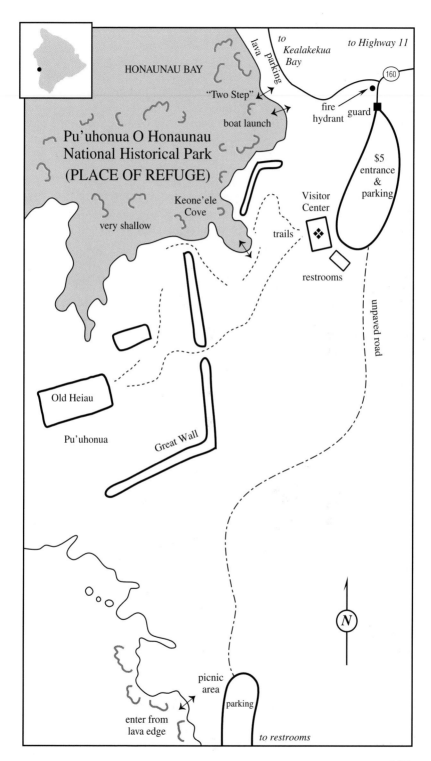

HONAUNAU BAY

to Kealakekua Bay

to Highway 11

160

lava parking

"Two Step"

boat launch

fire hydrant   guard

Pu'uhonua O Honaunau
National Historical Park
(PLACE OF REFUGE)

$5 entrance & parking

Keone'ele Cove

Visitor Center

very shallow

trails

restrooms

unpaved road

Old Heiau

Pu'uhonua

Great Wall

N

picnic area

parking

enter from lava edge

to restrooms

Picnic Area (south Place of Refuge)

Another terrific spot is on the opposite side of Place of Refuge in front of the picnic area. There's no beach here, just lava cliffs. It may not look easy to enter the water and isn't for beginners, but we found a fairly good lava entry (much like Two Step). Come early in the day for calmest conditions and be aware of any expected changes when snorkeling directly off a lava shore.

Park in the first picnic section, and walk across the black lava toward the water. Shoes or booties are essential when it's hot. At first glance, entry appears difficult, but look carefully and you'll find smooth sloping shelves that provide practical entry and exit (use caution—this is for experienced snorkelers only if there is much swell). Also, see Understanding Waves, page 27.

On calm days, getting out is easy, because you can look underwater for natural lava steps. Getting in simply involves pushing off from a lava ledge. This is another wonderful and different site because the lava forms sharp canyons. In places the adventuresome can let the currents sweep them through holes and narrow canyons (only for the brave with snorkeling buddies, as well as good health and disability insurance). Snorkel in either direction. If you swim quite a ways to the right (north), you can watch fish considering whether or not to nibble the fishing lines off the point. Water temperature changes are frequent here caused by the cool fresh water entering the sea.

GETTING THERE   Drive to the left of the information building at Place of Refuge (see area map, page 115). Instead of parking in the main lot, continue through to the far left of the parking onto a small road past two signs that say "picnic" and "no parking" (see site map, page 131). It angles to the right toward the water, but looks like it goes nowhere. Follow this road and you'll come upon a parking lot and picnic tables, with restrooms at the far end. Park here at the north end of the picnic area and walk straight toward the ocean across the smooth pahoehoe lava. Watch the swells carefully before entering the water and definitely leave a colorful bag so that you can find the same spot for your exit.

Picnic tables, shade and a lovely view are available here, but the restrooms and water are located at the end of the road to the south. Restrooms and water can also be found at the entrance to Place of Refuge. You will need shoes or flip-flops to cross the black lava on a hot summer day.

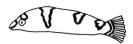

juvenile yellowtail coris

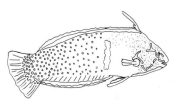

adult yellowtail coris

juvenile rockmover wrasse

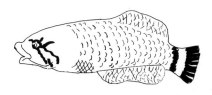

adult rockmover wrasse

Ho'okena Beach

Ho'okena is one of several more distant beaches south of Kona and around the southern tip of the island. Most of these can be snorkeled only in calm weather, so ask about conditions locally before trying them. Snorkeling conditions are dependent on the direction of the waves and can sometimes be fine even during stormy winter months when wind direction changes—sometimes quite suddenly.

Ho'okena is a nice sheltered bay with snorkeling on the left. It does have restrooms, showers, palms, some tidepools and boat entry, although the facilities are fairly basic and not always clean. Walking or driving to the right will take you to Kealia Beach which is poor for swimming, but good for snorkeling because of its wide, shallow coral shelf.

GETTING THERE   Driving south on Highway 11 (see map, page 115), go 2.6 miles past the Highway 160 turnoff, which heads for Place of Refuge. The Ho'okena turnoff is well-marked, so it's easy to find. Follow this paved road 2.3 miles toward the water at the end. It's only one and a half lanes wide and winding, but easy to drive.

Miloli'i Beach Park

For the public beach on Miloli'i Bay, just follow the signs to Miloli'i Beach Park. Snorkel here in calm weather only; there's lots to see right near the shore.

We've heard that Papa Bay just north has excellent snorkeling at the far right. We hesitated to try it because it's necessary to cross through the residential section to the right when you reach the bottom of the hill. Signs at each street to the right state "Private subdivision, not a public access, residents and authorized persons only, violators will be prosecuted". This neighborhood is Hawai'ian Lands and prefers its privacy. Snorkeling from a boat would be a better way to access this site.

GETTING THERE   On Highway 11 (see map, page 4), pass marker 89, then watch for the Miloli'i sign. The steep road down to the beach starts out as a newly-paved one-lane road, then becomes older and even narrower as it switches back and forth. It's about 5 miles down with some local traffic (uphill has the right-of-way), so go nice and slow.

If You Love the Reef

- Show respect for the reef creatures by causing them no harm.

- Avoid touching the coral, as touching kills it.

- Come as a respectful visitor rather than as a predator.

- Leave the many beautiful creatures you find there in peace so that others may enjoy them as you have.

- Allow the fish their usual diet rather than feeding them. Feeding them ultimately destroys their natural balance, and causes their numbers to decline. It also makes them more aggressive towards people, and can result in fish bites.

- Think of the creatures of the reef as fellow travelers in our life journey and then you may comprehend their magnificence.

- Join our reef Easter egg hunt: try to find and dive for at least one piece of trash on every snorkel, and take it away with you. It sharpens your eye, and if enough folks do it, it will be hard to find any. Don't try to clean up the whole world. Just pick up one or two things every time you're out.

- Use sunscreen less, and cover-ups more. Sunscreen dissolves in the water, and is toxic to fish and coral. A lycra body suit or a wetsuit takes care of most of your body better anyway, and costs less than sunscreen in the long haul. Save your sun screen for your sensitive face.

threadfin butterflyfish

Ka'u area (South Point)

The southern point of the Big Island is located in the Ka'u district. This interesting, windswept corner of the island is the most southerly land in all fifty states. While it isn't the Big Island's prettiest corner (for it is rather barren due to the strong winds), it's dramatic and worth the drive. Be sure to visit the high cliffs and ladders where ships used to be loaded.

Bays along this southern coast offer good snorkeling, but only when south swells aren't rolling in from the South Pacific. Check the weather report before counting on water sports of any kind along the south coast—especially in the summer. Mahana Bay (Green Sand Beach) is very exposed to the south, but worth the hike anyway. Just stay out of the water here if in doubt. Kaulana Bay is more protected, but not nearly as pretty.

Kaulana Bay

When the heat pick ups in the summer, Kaulana Bay is a nice place for a quick dip or snorkel when visiting the Ka Lae (South Point). Go when winds and surf are low. Although not the island's most picturesque spot, we enjoy the snorkeling in this small bay and have seen plenty—including a snowflake eel, Hawai'ian hogfish and huge schools of whiteband surgeonfish. Unfortunately, summer swells often hit from the south, so Kaulana can be dangerous just when you're in the mood to cool off. Stay within the points if in doubt about offshore currents. When calm, you'll see children playing near the ramp and their parents fishing from the sides.

Ample parking in the dirt lot at the edge of the water, but no facilities and no shelter from the sun. Restrooms available back at the visitor's center.

GETTING THERE   Take Highway 11 from Kailua-Kona toward the far south of the island. Turn right on South Point Road. Take a left at the visitor center rather than right toward the point. This road to the left will wind toward Kaulana Bay, where you can park anywhere on the dirt area next to the bay. This is the end of the road.

Entry is easiest from the old concrete boat ramp in the center, providing you don't slip on the algae. Snorkel anywhere within the bay, venturing beyond the points ONLY if you have exceptionally calm weather. Watch carefully for offshore currents in the deeper water beyond the points.

136

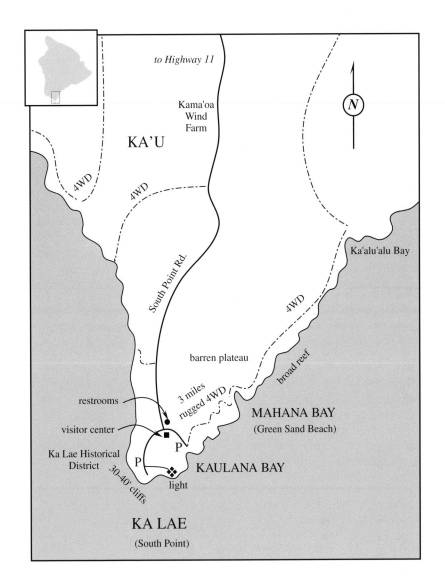

to Highway 11

Kama'oa
Wind
Farm

KA'U

N

4WD

4WD

South Point Rd.

Ka'alu'alu Bay

4WD

barren plateau

broad reef

3 miles
rugged 4WD

restrooms

visitor center

Ka Lae Historical
District

30-40' cliffs

P

P

light

MAHANA BAY
(Green Sand Beach)

KAULANA BAY

KA LAE
(South Point)

Moorish idol

Mahana Beach (Green Sands)

This beautiful and unusual beach can't be reached by anything you can rent from the regular car companies—not even 4WD. Some big local 4WD vehicles can make the trip over the deeply-rutted barren landscape, but just barely. There are some locals who make a business of shuttling people out there for a fee. It does make an interesting and beautiful trip.

If you're feeling energetic, hike the three miles over barren, windswept terrain passing interesting historical sites along the way—a great excuse to rest. Basically, all trails to the east lead to the same place. You can't miss Green Sands Beach. It's a dramatic crater, dropping down from the plateau, with greenish olivine sand and an enticing beach with good snorkeling and swimming when calm.

This is not the place for beginners unless seas are completely calm, but it's a delightful location when the weather is decent. Take rugged shoes, sun protection and plenty of water. After such a long hike, why not stay for a picnic too?

Green Sands is unique and has good snorkeling—especially to the left. Entry is easy from the sand as long as swells aren't too high. Swimmers and beginners should remain close to shore, but experienced snorkelers can wander around the rocks IF conditions are safe. Keep in mind that big south swells tend to arrive in the summer from storms in the South Pacific. And these big swells bring dangerous offshore currents.

Check on surf conditions before embarking on this hike, because it's a shame to trek three hot miles and not be able to play in this beautiful bay.

GETTING THERE   Head south from Kailua-Kona and take Highway 11 to the turnoff for South Point to the right. At the visitor center, take the Y to the left that leads to Kaulana Bay at the end of the road (see area map, page 137). Park here on the dirt and hike on the dirt road leading to the left (east) approximately three miles.

The trail has numerous branches as it passes the old stone walls, but stay fairly close to the water and you'll easily spot the dramatic green sand crater. Last time we were there, a pole marked the path down. The trail down to the beach is about 300 yards and not as difficult as it appears from the top. The beach is beautiful, but offers no shade in the middle of the day. Enter from the sand at the center of the beach and snorkel to the left and around the rocks as far as seems safe.

No facilities here. Restrooms are located back at the visitor center—rather basic, but open even when the center is closed.

138

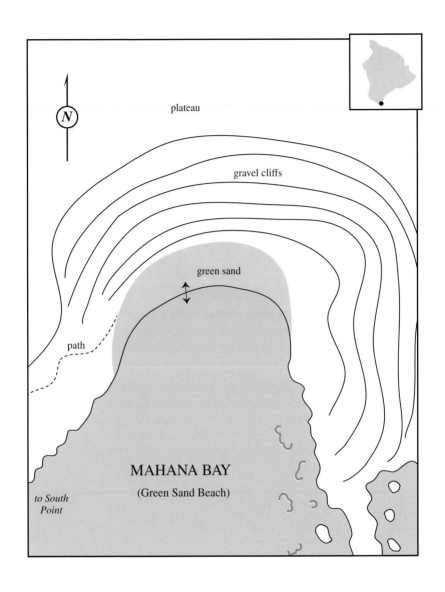

plateau

gravel cliffs

green sand

path

MAHANA BAY

(Green Sand Beach)

to South
Point

orangeband surgeonfish

Whittington Beach Park

Whittington Beach Park encompasses several lovely beaches with lots of picnic sites, facilities and tidepools. Most of the area is lava, so access is tricky, especially if there are any waves at all. Plenty of wind hits this southern part of the island.

The best spot to enter the water is just left of the old wharf (at the far right of the park), where the sea tends to be more protected. Swim around the wharf to the right and snorkel the rocks to the right of this small bay. The entry here over lava and coral is definitely not for beginners—especially when there are waves. Watch very carefully for the wind direction and currents. Ask local people for advice whenever possible; there are usually local families picnicking, and sometimes scuba diving groups.

Keep in mind that locals may find the place much easier than you do when there are swells because they've had more practice. It's not always as easy as you think to keep from getting scraped (or worse) on the coral when a wave suddenly arrives (see Understanding Waves, page 27). Portapotties are available, but no drinking water.

GETTING THERE   From Kailua-Kona, head south on Highway 11 past South Point (see map, page 4). Eventually the highway comes close to the water at Whittington, which is along the right. As you come down a hill and see water near the highway, watch carefully. There is a sign, but it's set about 25' off the highway, so it's easy to sail on by. You have to make a sharp right at the sign and double back about .25 of a mile to the parking area.

Punalu'u Beach Park (Black Sand Beach)

A pretty spot to stop on your way around the southern part of the Big Island, Punalu'u Beach Park offers showers, restrooms, camping, phone, even drinking water. The black-sand beach has a boat ramp at the northeastern end where you can enter the water, but only on a calm day. When winds and south swells pick up, stay close to shore because the current can be strong anywhere along the south coast. The rocky beach adds to the challenge.

GETTING THERE   As Highway 11 passes South Point and swings back toward Hilo, the highway passes close to Black Sand Beach. It's just to the north of Ninole (see map, page 4). Not a bad place to take a break on a trip to the volcano (if coming from the south). It's close to Highway 11, to the east of Whittington.

Doctor my Eyes

If you are swimming along snorkeling peacefully and your vision suddenly loses focus, don't be too quick to panic and call for a doctor. While you may have had a stroke or the water may be oily, there is a much more likely cause: You've probably just entered into an outdoor demonstration of the refractive qualities of mixtures of clear liquids of different densities. Is that perfectly clear?

Near the edge of some protected bays, clear spring water oozes smoothly out into the saltwater. As it is lighter than the mineral-laden saltwater, it tends to float in a layer near the surface for a time. When you swim into it, you'll often notice a sudden drop in the water temperature. The fresh spring water can be downright chilly.

Now, clear spring water is easy to see through, as is clear saltwater. If you mix them thoroughly, you have dilute saltwater, still clear. But when the two float side by side, the light going through them is bent and re-bent as it passes between them, and this blurs your vision. It's much like the blurring produced when hot, lighter air rises off black pavement, and produces wavy vision and mirage.

These lenses of clear water drift about, and often disappear as quickly as they appeared. Swimming away from the source of the spring water usually solves the problem. Clear at last?

Puna area

Puna, in the southeastern corner of the Big Island, is about as far as you can get from the major tourist areas, other than Hawai'i Volcanoes National Park. You may want to combine a visit to the volcanoes with a snorkeling break in a series of swimming-pool sized tidepools. The Puna area is scenic, has several large parks, and plenty to do. Visit the volcano area on your way; check out Lava Tree Monument; lunch in the small town of Pahoa; soak in the hot springs at Isaac Hale Beach Park (page 144); or snorkel in the tidepools at Wai'opae (page 146).

Consider staying through the evening in order to drive down Chain of Craters Road at sunset to see the flowing red-orange lava after dark. Check first with park rangers for the latest information as to whether any lava is flowing, and where you can park closest to it. If you're lucky, you may be able to hike across the hardened lava to see the newest lava up close. A truly unforgettable experience. At times the lava flow can best be reached from the Puna side of the flow. There is no road connecting the coast across this active flow.

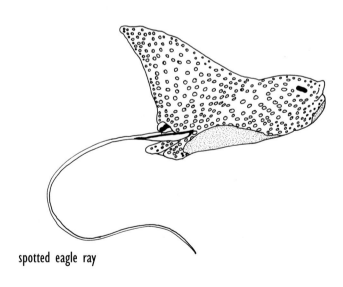

spotted eagle ray

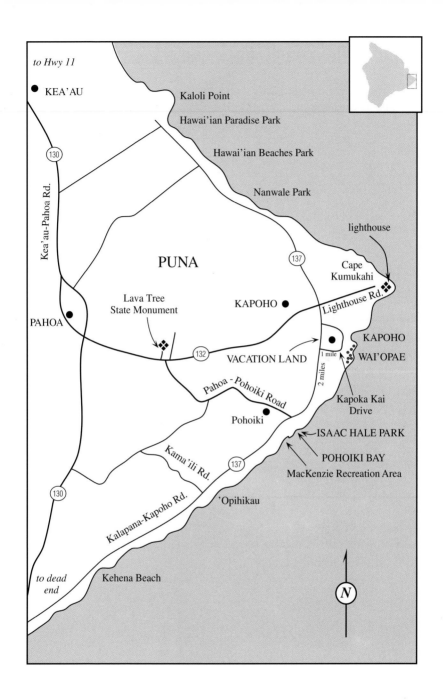

to Hwy 11

KEA'AU

Kaloli Point

Hawai'ian Paradise Park

Hawai'ian Beaches Park

Nanwale Park

130

Kea'au-Pahoa Rd.

lighthouse

PUNA

137

Cape
Kumukahi

Lava Tree
State Monument

KAPOHO

Lighthouse Rd.

PAHOA

132

KAPOHO
WAI'OPAE

VACATION LAND

1 mile

2 miles

Pahoa - Pohoiki Road

Kapoka Kai
Drive

Pohoiki

ISAAC HALE PARK

Kama'ili Rd.

137

POHOIKI BAY

130

MacKenzie Recreation Area

'Opihikau

Kalapana-Kapoho Rd.

to dead
end

Kehena Beach

N

Isaac Hale Beach Park (Pohoiki Bay)

On a calm day you can easily enter the water to snorkel at the popular boat ramp at Isaac Hale Beach Park. Watch carefully for boat traffic, which is frequent in the summer. Snorkel straight out into a very protected area.

If the sea is close to flat, you can snorkel to the left around the pier to venture further out. It's not really difficult snorkeling, but always requires fins even when it looks easy. When south swells pick up, you'll have to look it over carefully and keep in mind there can be a strong current in the center of the bay. Large south swells often create strong offshore currents.

This park is an attractive and popular place with lush surroundings to explore—including natural volcano-warmed fresh water pools in the lava. Facing the sea, a small path leads off towards the right to the pools, where warm water bubbles into the lava pools surrounded by jungle greenery. No showers or drinking water here, but plenty of sand beach.

GETTING THERE   Take Highway 11 (see area map, page 143) to Highway 130 (Kea'au-Pahoa Road). The intersection is at the town of Kea'au. Head south on Highway 130, a beautiful tree-lined drive with smooth pavement. At Pahoa, continue straight toward the water on Highway 132 through a lush overgrown area. Don't take the Lava Tree turnoff that you'll see on the left.

Just past the Lava Tree turnoff, hold to the right (holding left leads to Kapoho) on Pahoa-Pohoiki Road, which eventually narrows to one lane. You'll arrive at a wonderful large park (see site map, page 147). You can park on the right near the boat entry area at the breakwater, where it's calmest. It's a very short walk out on the little breakwater if you want to check out conditions from the end. Snorkel from the sandy beach to the left around the breakwater as far as it is calm. Always be alert for boat traffic as well as any offshore currents or riptides.

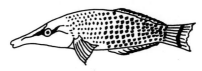

female bird wrasse

male bird wrasse

Wai'opae Tidepools

The Wai'opae tidepools area is at the Vacation Land development just west of Kapoho Bay—Kapoho means depression in Hawai'ian. This is a magical and unique place where you can snorkel in large interconnecting lava tidepools with unusual and very colorful coral with lots of smallish fish. The area is entirely protected by a long natural lava breakwater. In the tidepools, you'll see coral unique to this area, which makes it worth a side trip if you're over on this side of the island.

A local resident told us that visitors are welcome as long as they do not litter or damage their precious tidepools, which are still in excellent condition. We urge you to heed this local sentiment, and treat the tidepools with care.

The tidepools are completely protected by a large reef, getting no swell or currents other than the tide coming and going. Any junk that goes in, tends to stay in. "Take only pictures, and leave only footprints" would be a good idea here. If you find any litter, please take it out with you.

There are no facilities at all, so come prepared. Walk out over the lava wearing shoes (not flip-flops)—this is fairly rough lava and you will need to walk about 2/3 of the way toward the breaking waves, about two hundred yards. The first tidepools you see are quite shallow, but as you proceed, they become deeper and more interesting.

The best time to snorkel the tidepools is at high tide, because it's easier to glide from pool to pool then. Check which way the tide is going and follow it, rather than swimming against it.

Reef shoes or booties are better than fins here because they enable you to snorkel one pool, and then climb over to another—which is especially useful if the tide is low. Old athletic shoes or any kind of plastic shoes will suffice if you don't have any reef shoes.

Many folks wear fins, which definitely aren't needed since the pools are small (with a few bigger than swimming pools). It's a little slippery getting in and you need to watch for a few sea urchins, but once in, the snorkeling is easy and captivating. The coral is green, pink, and purple—the most colorful and unusual we've seen in Hawai'i. The water is clear, calm and only about 5' deep so you get a chance to examine the coral up close. This is ideal for beginners who have enough control to avoid touching the coral.

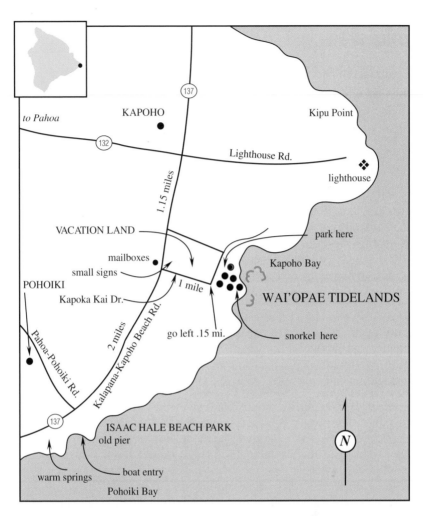

GETTING THERE From Isaac Hale (see map, page 143), take Highway 137 north about two miles until you see mailboxes on the left and a dirt road on the right (Kapoka Kai Road). Take a right here at a little sign that says "Vacation Land" and "private road". Continue one mile to the end of this road. When the road curves 90° at the water, take a left on an even smaller road (Wai'opae Road) for .15 mile until you can see the tidepools. Most folks park here under the "no parking" signs along with a few other cars.

From Kapoho, take 130 and follow the signs to Kapoho. Stay left on Highway 132 just past the Lava Tree exit. Kapoho also has excellent tidepools, but is private and has actually posted a guard, so you need to head south along the beach road (137) 1.15 miles until you see the cluster of mailboxes on the right, then take Kapoka Kai Rd. (a dirt road with a little sign that says "Vacation Land" and another "private road") to the left for 1 mile to the end, then a left on an even smaller road (Wai'opae Road) for .15 mile until you see the tidepools and park next to the no parking signs.

Hilo area

Dramatic Hilo, built mostly on black lava, used to be the most popular tourist destination on the Big Island. Set in the beautiful, jungle green, rainy side of Hawai'i, it is an area that seems in a time warp. Most tourists now prefer the sun-filled days on the leeward side of the island. Hilo is just the opposite in climate, getting rain 278 days a year. Hilo is still worth at least a day-trip, if only to see how lovely Hawai'i used to be.

You'll probably want to visit Hilo for other reasons, but there is good snorkeling available, weather permitting—especially at protected Richardson Beach Park (page 150). You do have to be prepared to snorkel in the rain, not a problem except that it can be a bit cooler over here. Since Hilo's beaches face the prevailing northeast trade winds, they need protection to be calm enough for either swimming or snorkeling. Exposed beaches are best for surfing.

If you drive to Hilo, be sure to spend some time in town. Shop a bit, stop for lunch, and enjoy the quieter atmosphere as well as the great beauty on this side of the island. Akaka Falls and the Hawai'i Tropical Botanical Garden (both north of Hilo) are just two of the attractions you won't want to miss.

Drive to Hilo either by way of Waimea or the Saddle Road (similar distance either way). While most car rental firms don't want you on the Saddle Road, it's a perfectly passable, but narrow, bumpy and bare road. It has no available gas or help should you have car trouble. Don't expect any sympathy or assistance from your car rental company if you break down up here. If you plan on going this way, you may want to allow time enough to make the long climb up to the top of Mauna Kea.

Money has been set aside for major improvements to the Saddle Road, but no one seems to know for sure when they will actually be done. Once the road work begins in earnest, the Saddle Road could be worse for some time. Any road work on this narrow road will slow you down.

milletseed butterflyfish

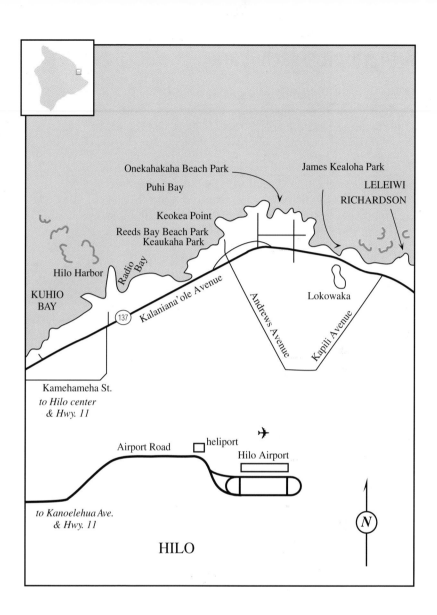

Onekahakaha Beach Park

Puhi Bay

James Kealoha Park

LELEIWI
RICHARDSON

Keokea Point

Reeds Bay Beach Park
Keaukaha Park

Hilo Harbor

Radio Bay

KUHIO
BAY

137

Kalaniana'ole Avenue

Andrews Avenue

Kapili Avenue

Lokowaka

Kamehameha St.
*to Hilo center
& Hwy. 11*

Airport Road   heliport

Hilo Airport

*to Kanoelehua Ave.
& Hwy. 11*

HILO

N

Richardson Beach Park

Many guides say that there is no snorkeling near Hilo. Not true. There is a row of similar shallow beaches very close to town—all of them along Kalanianaole Street (Highway 137) and very close together. Of the bunch, Richardson Park is definitely the best choice.

Snorkel near shore where entry is fairly easy over a tiny "beach". You can snorkel either direction. The large, near-shore area is well-protected by the outer reef, where the surfers play. In Hilo you will likely get to snorkel in the rain; so enjoy the raindrops on the surface of the water.

The water can be a bit cooler here due to fresh water springs common at many Big Island snorkeling sites. Patches of fresh water are also the cause of the patches of oily-looking water (see Doctor my Eyes, page 141). Just keep swimming and the temperature and clarity will change. Visibility tends to be worse on this side, due to the heavier swell action and rainwater runoff. If you hit a patch of weather that turns this side relatively calm, and you are in Hilo, give it a try. It's not worth a special trip from Kona, but fun if you're here.

This is not a beach for a person who likes to keep some space between their body and the coral. Most of it is quite shallow, especially at low tide. There's actually enough clearance, but not for the claustrophobic. One day, when we were snorkeling here, we had the lifeguard to ourselves. He enjoyed telling us more about the many fish we had seen and seemed genuinely happy to have some visitors.

If you just want a cooling dip, the other nearby beaches are mostly fine. The tidepools look inviting, but some are no longer clean, and have posted signs warning you to keep out.

A refreshing swim and shower are welcome, especially if you've driven all the way from Kailua-Kona to see the Hilo area. Don't let a little rain keep you from trying this pretty spot.

GETTING THERE   Cross the island to Hilo (see map, page 149). From the corner of Highway 11 and Kalanianaole Street. (the northwest corner of the Hilo Airport), take Kalanianaole Street. east along the shore. Drive 3.7 miles, passing Reed Bay, Puhi, Onekahakaha, Leleiwi, all with lots of tidepools and shallow reef.

Park in the little Richardson parking lot and walk toward the water. Showers and restrooms are available on the left close to the parking lot. Just behind the house continue walking to the right until you see the hidden lifeguard station. It's not far at all, just hidden by the vegetation.

Hamakua area

North of Hilo, the going gets slow as you head toward the end of the road that dead-ends when it reaches Waipio Valley. The northeastern section of the Big Island is not traversed by road—the valleys cut through too sharply. The biggest valley of this series is Waipio Valley. This lovely valley can only be reached from a very steep road by way of the town of Kukuihaele, where excursions are available for tourists.

Waipio Beach can have decent snorkeling when weather permits, but that's very rare, since the rugged north coast catches heavy north swells much of the year. Besides, coral growth is limited in areas that catch the brunt of northeastern swells. You're better off spending your time touring the lush jungle valley with its twin 1200-foot waterfalls.

If you've come to Hamakua, at least drive to the end of the road, where you can view this dramatic valley. Most of Hamakua is bordered by high cliff allowing little water access, but offers delightful views from the highway when the sky is clear.

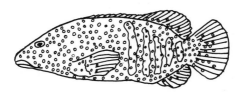

peacock grouper

WATER EXCURSIONS

Fair Wind II

The premier way to get to the beautiful Captain Cook Monument area, Fair Wind II is a custom-made, comfortable catamaran. It can easily hold up to 100 passengers without feeling crowded. The monument area (tucked into the NE corner of Kealakekua Bay) is nearly always calm, so trips are rarely cancelled. Departure is from the Keauhou Harbor, south of Kailua-Kona (see map, page 111).

Fair Wind II offers a variety of trips, and selection changes with the weather and season. The deluxe 4.5 hour trip is usually offered with both morning and afternoon departures. Sometimes there is instead a shorter snack trip in the afternoon. We always prefer mornings for the calm sea, but the afternoon trip costs less and Kealakekua Bay itself rarely gets much chop.

Fair Wind has special permission to keep a mooring in Kealakekua Bay, one of the best snorkeling sites in Hawai'i (see page 116). Continental breakfast and a filling lunch are available on their morning trip. Snacks, lunch, water slide, and all equipment are provided. SCUBA and Snuba® are available at an extra charge. Since the morning trip stays near the monument for several hours, you will have time for another snorkel after lunch.

This is a family operation that has been in business for 25 years. The boat and gear are all first rate and the employees work hard to make sure everyone has a great time.

What you see at the monument can vary, but it's nearly always clear and calm, with a good variety of fish. Sometimes you'll be lucky and see spinner dolphins cavorting in the center of the bay. Other creatures, such as rays, can also be spotted along the deeper edge of the reef. Watch carefully in the shallow areas near shore as well as the edge of the reef as it descends into the deep blue of the bay.

Fair Wind and others also offer rafting trips that make shorter, more frequent stops. These zodiac-type rafts are for the adventuresome, who enjoy the smaller group as well as the bouncy ride. Fair Wind offers plenty of fun—especially for families.

78-7130 Kaleiopapa St., Kailua-Kona 96740
(808) 332-2788   (800) 677-9461   fax (808) 324-1772

fairwind@interpac.net   web site: www.fair-wind.com

Children (6-17) get a reduced rate; age 5 and under are free.

Body Glove

Body Glove works hard at being the best known Kailua-Kona snorkeling excursion. You'll see ads for them everywhere, promoting their daily trips. Body Glove departs from the pier in Kailua-Kona, but uses a van for check-in. They will tell you how to find the pier parking area just up from Ali'i near the church, and where to meet the van.

Continental breakfast is available on the way out, with sandwiches served at the site. Sites will vary, but they usually go up the coast to the north. A popular site is just north of Old Airport. They provide all equipment, are friendly and enthusiastic, and offer SCUBA and Snuba® as an extra.

With a relatively short travel time, there is plenty of time to spend in the water. This area along the coast can have some swells, so check with them on conditions if you're concerned about snorkeling in surge conditions. Most excursions rarely miss a trip due to weather, so be prepared to come if you've made reservations.

(808) 326-7122   (800) 551-8911

web site: www.snorkelkona.com

Children age 5-17 are about half price; under age 5 are free.

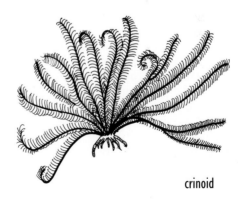

crinoid

Sea Adventures

If you're looking for excursions in the South Kohala area, try the Boathouse at Mauna Lani. It's located south of the Mauna Lani Bay Hotel, but run by the Orchid at Mauna Lani. Their ship, Winona, is at anchor off the little sand beach south of the historic fishponds.

They offer full snorkeling and diving programs, including SCUBA certification, whale watching (in season), sunset cruises, and charter excursions. We snorkel with them on the outer reef at Puako and thoroughly enjoy the trips. While Puako can be shore-accessed when conditions are very calm (see page 70), boats such as Winona provide safe access much of the year.

Snacks and all equipment are provided. Just bring your own towel. The Boathouse is open 8-5. While primarily provided for Mauna Lani Resort guests, they are happy to include others when space permits. Their "house reef" is excellent—a great alternative if the boat is full (see page 76).

(808) 885-7883

From the Orchid, call extension 7570 or the concierge at 7320.

Big Island Water Sports

This family-oriented outfit offers a full range of adventure excursions including snorkeling, SCUBA, Snuba®, whale watching (in season), and kayaking. They are friendly and flexible, with plenty of patience, so offer a chance to learn these skills from helpful crew members. It's unusual for a dive boat to encourage snorkelers, but this group will tailor a trip to the needs of each group of people.

They usually operate out of Honokohau Harbor (see map, page 83), which is convenient to either Kona or South Kohala and has ample parking with all facilities. They use smaller dive boats that hold fewer than 20 people, unlike the big excursion boats that carry as many as 100 people.

We tried their Snuba option from the boat Diversity at a site near the airport called Garden Eel Cove. By being able to go down 20 feet with Snuba gear, we could see the small garden eels on the 30 feet deep sandy floor. They have a wide variety of sites from which to choose, both north and south of the harbor. Dive boats will choose the best site upon departure, depending on the passengers interests as well as the water conditions.

We appreciated having comfortable equipment—especially soft weights. This was not a fancy lunch trip, but had enough snacks and drinks to keep us going. While we didn't need the lessons ourselves, we were impressed with how helpful and thorough they were. We would recommend them highly for families who want individual attention—especially for young children.

Snuba® is available for ages eight and older, while a new form, Snuba Doo, is available to any child at least four—providing they are comfortable in the water and know how to swim. Snuba Doo provides vests that keep the kids on the surface, where they learn to breathe through the regulator. This is a good first step toward Snuba, which takes you down as much as twenty feet. It's wonderful to see how fast children take to diving! All equipment is provided.

(808) 324-1650   fax (808) 324-4719

fun@bigislandwatersports.com   web site:
snuba@bigisland.com

seastar

Kohala Divers

With offices up north at Kawaihae Harbor (see page 45), this dive program has been in operation over twenty years and provides excellent trips for both divers and snorkelers. Staff members are friendly and fun while making sure everyone is safe and comfortable. They tailor each trip to the abilities of the day's passengers.

Two snorkeling excursions depart right off the beach from the Outrigger Hotel on 'Anaeho'omalu Bay ("A" Bay), where they have a dive shop on the north end of the beach. There are a variety of excellent sites available near here, so they choose the one that has the best conditions on a given day.

Their much smaller dive boats depart from Kawaihae Harbor (see map, page 45) near their main office. They welcome snorkelers on these dive trips, but may bump them if divers need the space on these smaller boats. Since they often head north along the coast, this is an excellent opportunity if they have space for snorkelers. The boat is usually a short swim from the edge of the rocky coast where you'll find some pristine snorkeling with excellent visibility and a great variety of fish and coral.

The underwater terrain in this area is quite varied with canyons, tiny coves, peninsulas of coral jutting out into the sea, and tall coral heads (see page 54). Since there are no beaches or resorts, the water is unusually clear. A small cliff (10-30') blocks access to the water along much of North Kohala, so it helps to have boat access.

(808) 882-7774   fax (808) 82-1536   h2osport@kohaladivers.com

Kawaihae Shopping Center, Kawaihae (near harbor)

Night manta viewing

Before the Kona Surf Resort (south of the Keauhou Harbor) was sold, they used to shine lights into the water to attract plankton that the manta ray love to eat at night. Dive boats would take people out to dive or snorkel with these huge creatures. It was an unforgettable experience that we would highly recommend. Hopefully, the new owners will light the same area, and the mantas will return.

Another night manta hangout is up north at the Mauna Kea Resort in South Kohala. Here you can even snorkel from the sandy shore to the bright light at the northern side, but will also need to provide your own waterproof lights. It's a bit cooler at night, so wear that wetsuit if you have one—especially in the winter.

When the huge mantas arrive, they do swoop through the water, constantly scooping up plankton guided by the little flaps on either side of the mouth. They like to move into the brightest spot in hope of finding plenty of plankton, so bring the brightest lights you have. When a mantas comes to share your light, you'll be able to see right into its large mouth. Impressive, to say the least. Mantas never harm people and can easily maneuver in spite of their large size. You MUST try this once. Unforgettable!

Kona Coast Divers

Jim Robertson operates Kona Coast Divers from his well-stocked store conveniently located in Kailua-Kona. While it primarily serves divers, there are certain trips that are appropriate for experienced snorkelers. Check with the store for details. As with other dive boats, lunch is served and equipment is provided, but without the frills of the larger excursions that cater to snorkelers.

75-5614 Palani Road, Kailua-Kona 96740

(808) 329-8802   (800) 562-3483

Atlantis

This is a submarine experience rather than a snorkeling one, but gives you a chance to see what's under the water without actually getting wet. Departs from the Kailua-Kona Pier with transfer to the submarine out in the bay. The trip takes about an hour total. The submarine dives down to 130 feet beneath the surface. A fun ride and an educational experience.

(808) 329-6626

Kailua Bay Glassbottom Boat Cruises

Kailua Bay provides a less expensive way to see the underwater world than Atlantis. A semi-submersible, rather than a submarine, the ship has larger windows for fish-viewing. You'll have a chance to see just how much coral and fish are right there in the pier area without getting wet. Departing from the Kailua-Kona Pier.

(808) 324-1749

Inflatable rafts

Bouncy and fast, these rafts (often called Zodiac®, a popular brand), designed for about ten people, provide a fun way to see a range of sites on one trip. In order to see a number of sites, each stop is usually short (about 15-30 minutes). Still, they do give you a chance to check out several sites and get a great view along the way.

Most have no shade or bathroom, so plan ahead. While inflatables are safe and comfortable as you ride on the air-filled sides and hold on to the rope, they are too bouncy for pregnant women or anyone with serious back problems. When seas are kicking up, they can provide quite a thrilling ride. Expect to get a bit wet if not completely soaked. You'll probably want your camera, so take a water-proof covering of some sort–for it and anything else you want to stay dry.

Kayaking

The Big Island is an excellent place to give kayaks a try even if you've never done so, since many large bays are calm most of the year. Kayaks are available in Kailua-Kona as well as along the highway in both South Kohala and South Kona.

The price of a kayak for the day or the week includes life vests, and attachment of the kayak to the top of your rental car. The typical kayak that is rented is a sit-on-top type. They're broad, stable and made of strong plastic and accommodate one or two adults in chair-like seats. They're heavy enough that you won't want to carry them very far from your car.

If you've kayaked before, and want to try something novel, many kayak rental shops will rent you a high-tech kayak at a higher charge. It's fun to at least look over the sleek ocean-going kayaks with steerable rudders, narrow efficient profiles, and lightweight construction. It's amazing how light a carbon fiber kayak can be. These are the kayaks you want to paddle if you're heading long distances, but not if you're going to encounter waves.

A popular, easy kayak trip is one mile across Kealakekua Bay from the pier at Napo'opo'o. See page 121 for the entry point and page 117 for the Captain Cook Monument on the other side of the wide, calm bay. If you're lucky, the pods of spinner dolphins will be cavorting in the middle of the bay. There's a nice, shallow cove just west of the monument where you can pull in with the kayak and enjoy a picnic lunch near the excellent snorkeling. Look here for the usually-submerged bronze plaque commemorating Captain Cook's demise– on your right as you pull into the former canoe-launching area.

Another popular kayak entry is from Kekaha Kai State Park north of Kailua-Kona. When seas are fairly calm, you can kayak north along this lovely coast, stopping for a secluded picnic and a snorkel at one of the pretty bays like Makalawena (see page 91).

Much of the western coast of the Big Island offers good kayaking when seas are calm, so this is a wonderful way to explore. Take your snorkeling gear and try some sites that are more difficult to reach by land. The harbors (Keauhou, Kailua, Honokohau, and Kawaihae) all offer excellent kayak entries and all facilities.

Kayaking opens up many sites for snorkeling that cannot be accessed safely from shore. If you're a good strong paddler, you can take yourself to many of the spots that excursion boats go. In fact, if you are out paddling, and see a boat discharge their snorkelers, check out that area yourself.

There are four obvious ways to kayak snorkel. The first is to paddle to a beach at a known good spot, pull in, secure your kayak well above the high tide, and snorkel away.

The second is to go out with a partner and take turns. One in the water, while the other follows and paddles. This is a good choice when you're unsure of the swell, or the swell is a little higher than you feel comfortable with.

The third is for advanced snorkelers. Paddle to a good spot, and tow the kayak behind you. A few precautions are wise. We like to tie the kayak tow rope to a wrist, because if your kayak were to drift away, you might not be able to swim fast enough to catch it. You also must be extra alert and cautious so that you don't drift into the break zone, and get dragged in as your kayak surfs the waves. Be careful if winds are high or swell is big. We've done some really interesting snorkeling this way.

The fourth is to paddle to a spot with an mooring buoy and tie up to it. There are public moorings and private moorings. You won't be able to tell which are which, but if it is not in use, it's OK. If a boat arrives and asks you to move, do so immediately.

The fifth and unspeakable alternative is to tie up to coral. Don't even consider it! Even touching coral damages it.

Kayaking subjects you to a lot of UV, so plan accordingly. A big broad hat helps but it doesn't block bounced light off the water. A lycra suit is great in warm weather. A wetsuit can be good in the winter, although if you're paddling much, it can be way too warm. You will still need sunscreen for your face.

LAND EXCURSIONS

Mauna Kea Summit Adventures

There's no snorkeling up here at more than 13,000 feet above sea level, but a nice contrast to water activities. If you've had enough time at the beach, consider letting Mauna Kea Summit Adventures take you to the highest ground in Hawai'i for a guided tour complete with heavy jackets, hot chocolate, and sandwiches.

We were very impressed with the knowledge of our expert guide, who answered questions non-stop from the time we left the South Kohala area at 2:45 pm until our return after 10 pm. He took us to within yards of the peak, showed us the observatories, gave us a half-hour stay to acclimatize at the little store at 9,000 feet, and finished by setting us a telescope to allow us to see numerous stars and planets in the crystal-clear sky.

We did appreciate the warm jackets, since the temperature was about 30 degrees F. with wind. Just a typical evening on the summit. Later in the week, the mountain was capped by snow. Take even more layers if you happen to have them!

While this is a very long drive, the MKSA vans are roomy and comfortable, and there is plenty to see and talk about on the way. The vans are equipped with a headset for the driver and speakers, so it's easy for everyone.

While it's possible to drive your car all the way (unless it has just snowed), this is a long, bumpy trip. The road is quite serviceable, but steeper than anything you're used to at home, and it's hard on the brakes coming down. Your car rental company would not be happy to get a call from here. Most folks don't have the clothes needed to enjoy their time on top anyway. It would be a shame to drive all that way up there and be unable to set foot outside your car due to the wind chill!

Warning to divers: don't go up in the mountains within 24 hours of your last dive unless you want to fizz like a glass of cola.

(808) 322-2366   (888) 322-2366 (toll free)

www.maunakea.com

Waipio Valley Wagon Tours

Waipio Valley is a lush, relatively untouched remnant of old Hawai'i. If you come to Hamakua, Waipio is well worth a visit down. You can either park at the overlook, or go on down into the valley. The road into the valley is paved, but too steep for two wheel drive vehicles. Waipio Valley Wagon Tours offers an interesting, moderately priced 1 1/2-hour tour of the lower part of the valley by mule-drawn wagon. Drive to the Last Chance Store in the small town of Kukuihaele along the highway in Hamakua, north of Hilo to meet their shuttle van. They operate Monday through Saturday, with rides departing at 9:30, 11:30, 1:30 and 3:30. Reservations are a good idea.

You descend the steep road by 4WD van, with a descriptive talk along the way. Then you board a quaint horse-driven carriage for the tour, pulled by a team of two huge draft mules. When there's been recent rain (which is typical), you will see slender twin 1200-foot waterfalls along the valley rim. Traditional taro farming is still the dominant crop in the valley. While there are an increasing number of homes these days, most have no electricity or running water.

(808) 775-9518

Last Chance Store in Kukuihaele, Hamakua

Helicopters

Numerous companies offer helicopter tours of the Big Island. If money isn't an issue, it's lots of fun. Due to the size of the Big Island, some trips are quite long and costly. The views of the volcanoes, the northern valleys, and anywhere along the coast are truly spectacular from the air. Packages of varying length are available, starting at about $99 and going up to much, much more.

Weather must cooperate, so be prepared to reschedule should the east side of the island be too cloudy or stormy. If you are driving from a distance, be sure to confirm your flight right before you leave the hotel to save a long disappointing drive. Flights depart from Keahole Airport, South Kohala, and Hilo.

If you ever get motion sickness, be prepared (see page 93). The air can be quite choppy flying over the wide expanses of lava flows. If your main purpose is to see Volcanoes Park, it's worth driving to Hilo and buying a shorter, less expensive flight there. Even by helicopter, it's quite a long haul to Volcanoes Park from South Kohala or Keahole Airport.

Hawai'i Volcanoes National Park

The Big Island is home to Kilauea, one of the most active volcanoes in the world. Kilauea has been pouring out lava almost continually for the past 300,000 years. Its most recent eruption began in 1983, and has gone on pretty much non-stop since then. In 1989, it buried the coastside visitors center. In 1990 it flowed right on through the community of Kalapana, destroying 100 homes as it laid down a 75-foot deep lava flow. This is not a volcano to mess with!

When lava is flowing, Hawai'i Volcanoes National Park offers an exciting chance to be near Kilauea's flow toward the sea. No one knows how long the Big Island will keep growing as it builds more land along the southern coast. Nearly a square mile of land area has been added by lava flow into the sea just since 1983. For more details about Big Island geology, see page 178.

Stop at the visitor center to watch their excellent video and hear the day's weather and lava report. Crater Rim Road is a good start for a tour—especially is you've brought a warm jacket, because it's usually cool at this elevation and often rainy.

After visiting the upper park area with its many interesting short hikes, consider staying long enough to view the lava after dark. Chain of Craters Road twists slowly down the hill to the sea, where you can park at the end of the road ($5) and walk to the current viewpoint (if accessible from this side—check with park rangers first). This flow changes, so the best access is sometimes reached from the end of the road in Puna.

You'll see dramatic black-sand beaches built recently and often can see the molten red lava on the hill as it flows toward the sea, but will seldom have a chance to view lava fountains. Rangers are available to answer your questions and guide you to the best viewing areas safely. This is a long drive from Kona or Kohala, but well worth the trip when the lava flows down the hill into the sea or sprays high into the air. Fortunately, the long highways are well-maintained, with little traffic away from the western towns. Drag yourself out of the water at least once to see this magnificent park.

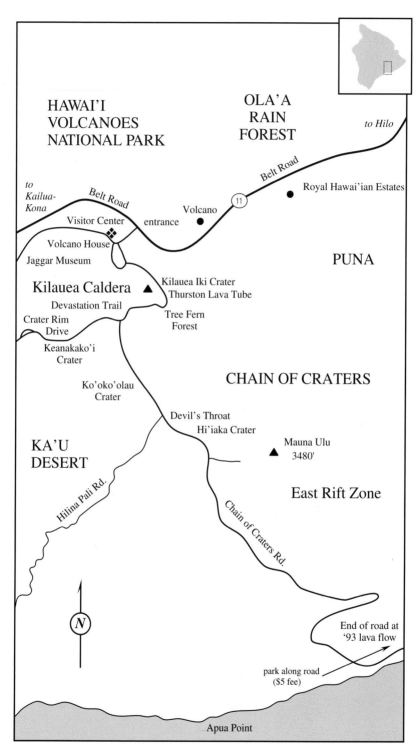

HAWAI'I
VOLCANOES
NATIONAL PARK

OLA'A
RAIN
FOREST

to Hilo

to
Kailua-
Kona

Belt Road

Belt Road

11

Volcano

Royal Hawai'ian Estates

Visitor Center

entrance

Volcano House

PUNA

Jaggar Museum

Kilauea Caldera ▲

Kilauea Iki Crater
Thurston Lava Tube

Devastation Trail

Tree Fern
Forest

Crater Rim
Drive

Keanakako'i
Crater

CHAIN OF CRATERS

Ko'oko'olau
Crater

Devil's Throat
Hi'iaka Crater

Mauna Ulu ▲
3480'

KA'U
DESERT

East Rift Zone

Hilina Pali Rd.

Chain of Craters Rd.

N

End of road at
'93 lava flow

park along road
($5 fee)

Apua Point

163

Marine Life

The coral reef supports tremendous diversity in a small space. On a healthy reef, you've never seen everything, because of the boggling variety of species, as well as changes from day to day and changes from day to night. The reef functions much like the oasis in the desert providing food (more abundant than the open ocean) and shelter from predators. Only the wild rain forests can compare with the reef in complexity.

In Hawai'i the reef coral itself is less spectacular than in warmer waters of the world. This is counterbalanced by the colorful and abundant fish, which provide quite a show.

There are excellent color fish identification cards available in bookstores and dive shops. We particularly like the ones published by Natural World Press. There are also many good marine life books that give far more detailed descriptions of each creature than we attempt in these brief notes.

OCTOPUS

Some varieties of octopuses hide during the day; others will hunt for food then. They eat shrimp, fish, crabs, and mollusks—you should eat so well! Octopuses have strong "beaks" and can bite humans, so it's safer to not handle them.

Being mollusks without shells, they must rely on speed, cunning and camouflage to escape danger. Octopuses are capable of imitating a flashing sign, or changing their color and texture to match their surroundings in an instant. This makes them very hard to spot, even when they're hiding in plain sight— usually on the bottom or on rocks. They also squirt an ink to confuse predators or prey. They live about two years.

Just because you haven't seen one does not mean they aren't there. Go slow and watch carefully for the "rock" that moves.

REEF SQUID

These graceful, iridescent creatures hang around reef areas, often forming a single long line. All eyes will follow you easily since they have 360 degree vision. They can capture surprisingly large fish with their tentacles.

SHRIMP

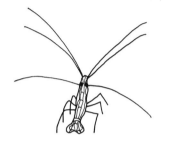

In all kinds, colors, and sizes, they like to hide in rocks and coral—often living symbiotically with the coral. They are difficult to spot during the daytime, but at night you will notice lots of tiny pairs of eyes reflected in the flashlight beam. Most are fairly small and well-disguised.

Some examples include: the harlequin shrimp (brightly colored) that eat sea stars, the banded coral shrimp (found all over the world), and numerous tiny shrimp that you won't see without magnification.

SEA URCHINS

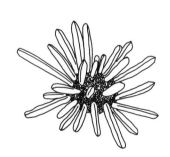

Concealed tube feet allow urchins to move around in their hunt for algae.The collector urchin has pebbles and bits of coral attached for camouflage. These urchins are quite common in Hawai'i, and have no spines.

Beware of purple-black urchins with long spines. These are common in shallow water at certain beaches. It's not the long spines that get you, it's the ones beneath. The bright red pencil sea urchin is common and easy to spot. Although large, its spines aren't sharp enough to be a problem for people.

CRINOIDS

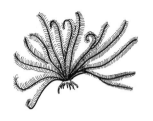

These animals seen on top of the rocks or coral can easily be mistaken for plants. They are sometimes called "feather stars" and are delicate and beautiful plankton feeders.

SEA STARS

Abundant, in many colors and styles. The crown of thorns sea star, which can be such a devastator of coral reefs, is found in Hawai'i, but not in large numbers like the South Pacific. Sea stars firmly grasp their prey with strong suction cups, and then eat at leisure.

RAYS

Manta rays (large plankton-eaters) use two flaps to guide plankton into their huge efficient mouths. Mantas often grow to be two meters from wing-tip to wing-tip, and can weigh 300 pounds. They can't sting, but are large enough to bump hard.

Mantas feed at night by doing forward rolls in the water with mouths wide open. Lights will attract plankton which appeal to the manta rays. Dive boats in favored locations can easily attract them with their bright lights making the night trips quite exciting.

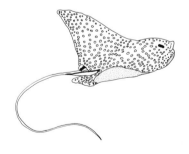

Another beautiful ray, the spotted eagle ray, can sometimes be seen cruising the bottom for food and can grow to be seven feet across. They have a dark back with lots of small white dots and an extremely long tail. Their fins function more like wings to enable them to "fly" along rather than swimming.

Common sting rays prefer the sandy bottom and stay in calm, shallow, warmer water.

EELS

Many types of moray eels abound among the reefs of Hawai'i. They can easily grow up to two meters long.

Varieties of moray found in Hawai'i include whitemouth, snowflake, zebra (black and white stripes), wavy-lined, mottled, and dragon moray (often reddish-brown with distinct white spots of differing sizes).

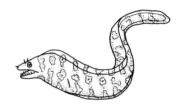

Morays prefer to hide in holes during the day. If out cruising, they often find a nearby hole when spotting a snorkeler. When they stick out their heads and breathe, their teeth are most impressive.

Eels generally have no interest in eating snorkelers, other than very annoying ones, while they are quite happy and able to swallow a fairly large fish.

TRUMPETFISH

These long, skinny fish can change color, often bright yellow or light green—and will change right in front of your eyes. They sometimes hang upright to blend with their environment, lying in wait to suck in their prey. Sometimes they shadow another fish to sneak up on prey—even at a cleaning station.

They do eat during the day, which is unusual for fish-eaters, who usually eat at dawn or dusk. Trumpetfish are quite common in Hawai'i and often seen alone. Some grow to more than one meter long.

NEEDLEFISH

These pointed, common silvery-blue fish like swimming very near the surface, usually in schools— occasionally leaping from the water. All types of needlefish are long and skinny

167

as their name implies, and grow to as much as 1-2 feet long. Color and markings vary, but the long narrow shape is distinctive and hard to mistake. They're usually bluish on top, and translucent below for camouflage.

BUTTERFLYFISH

Butterflyfish are beautiful, colorful, abundant and varied in Hawai'i. They have incredible coloration, typically bright yellow, white, orange, black, and sometimes a little blue. They hang out near coral, eating algae, sponges, tube worms and coral polyps. No one really understands the purpose of their beautiful colors, but many have speculated. Perhaps they serve territorial needs.

Juveniles are often distinctly different in coloring. Bizarre patterns may confuse predators—especially since they can pivot fast. Bars may help some hide, while stripes are seen more in faster fish. Black lines across the eyes and spots near the tail also confuse predators.

Butterflyfish are often seen in pairs remaining together for up to three years. They're delightful to watch. Hovering and turning are more important to them than speed since they stay near shelter of the reef and catch a quick meal—like a tube worm.

The ones you are most likely to see in Hawai'i include: raccoon (reminding you of the face of the animal), ornate (with bright orange lines making it easy to spot), threadfin (another large, beautiful one), saddleback, lemon (very tiny), bluestripe (a beautiful one found only in Hawai'i), fourspot, milletseed, oval, teardrop, and forceps (also called long nose). The lined butterflyfish is the largest variety found in Hawai'i.

Many butterflyfish have black spots near the tail—perhaps to confuse a predator about which way they're headed. Watch and they may confuse you too.

PARROTFISH

Among the most dramatically colored fish on the reef, male parrotfish are blue, green, turquoise, yellow, lavender, and/or orange with endless variations of these colors. Females tend to be reddish brown. No two are alike. Parrotfish are very beautiful, with artistic, abstract markings.

These fish change colors at different times in their lives and can also change sex as needed. They can be quite large (up to one meter).

Patient grazers, they spend countless hours scraping algae from dead coral with their large, beak-like teeth, and create tons of white sand in the process. Most prefer to zoom away from snorkelers, but you'll see them passing gracefully by and will hear them crunching away at the coral.

TRIGGERFISH

Fond of sea urchins as a main course, triggerfish graze during the day on algae, worms and other small items.

Varieties include the Picasso (wildly colorful—not too many at each beach, but worth watching for), reef (the Hawai'ian state fish), pinktail (easy to identify with its black body, white fins and pink tail), black (common, distinctive white lines between body and fins). The checkerboard triggerfish has a pink tail, yellow-edged fins, and blue stripes on its face. All triggerfish are very beautiful and fascinating to watch.

FILEFISH

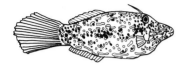

The scrawled filefish has blue scribbles and brown dots over its olive green body. Quite large, up to one meter, often in pairs, but seen occasionally in groups.

A filefish will often turn its body flat to your view, and raise its top spine in order to impress you. This lets you have a great close-up view—a perfect photo opportunity.

The brown filefish (endemic) is much smaller, with lines on its head and white spots on its brown body. The fantail filefish (also endemic and small) has a distinct orange tail and lots of black spots over a light body. Filefish will sometimes change color patterns rapidly for camouflage.

SURGEONFISH

Razor-sharp fin-like spines on each side of the tail are the hallmark of this fish, quite common in Hawai'i. These spines provide excellent defense, but aren't needed to fend off tourists since surgeonfish can easily swim away.

Varieties includes the orangeband surgeonfish (with distinctive long, bright orange marks on the side), as well as the Achilles tang (also called naso tang), which has bright orange spots surrounding the spines near the orange tail. The yellow tang is completely yellow and smaller. The sailfin tang has dramatic vertical markings. It's less common, but easy to identify.

WRASSES

Wrasses are amazingly bright and multicolored fish. Some very small ones set themselves up for business and operate a cleaning station, where they clean much larger fish without having to worry about becoming dinner. They eat parasites, and provide an improbable reef service in the process. Perhaps their bright colors serve as neon signs to advertise their services Hang out near their cleaning stations for excellent fish viewing. In Hawai'i, the cleaner wrasse is bright yellow, purple and black.

Other wrasses are large including the dazzling yellowtail (up to 15 inches), which has a red body covered with glowing blue spots, a few stripes, and a bright yellow tail.

Another large wrasse, the saddleback, is endemic to Hawai'i. It is bright blue, with green and orange markings. Wrasses are closely related to parrotfish. Like parrotfish, they can change colors and sex.

SCORPIONFISH

This improbable-looking fish is very colorful, with feather-like multicolor spines. Beware of their poisonous spines, though! Don't even think about touching a scorpionfish, and try to avoid accidentally stepping on one.

This varied group of exotic fish includes the bright red Hawai'ian turkeyfish, sometimes called a lionfish.

Others are so well-camouflaged that they are hard to see. They just lurk on the bottom blending in well with the sand and coral. If you see one, count yourself lucky.

PUFFERFISH

Pufferfish (and the related trunkfish) swim slowly, so need more protection. Some can blow up like balloons when threatened.

Two kinds are common in sheltered areas: porcupine (displaying spines when inflated), and spotted trunkfish and boxfish (often brown or black with lots of white dots). They tend to prefer to escape under the coral, although some seem unafraid of snorkelers.

SHARKS

Although sharks have quite a reputation for teeth rather than brains, they are unquestionably survivors, having been around for about 300 million years.

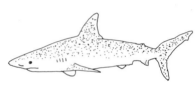

This is an extremely successful species with keen hearing, smell, sight and ability to detect electrical signals through the water. They swim with a side-to-side motion, which does not make them speedy by ocean standards.

When snorkeling you are unlikely to spot any shark except the reef or white-tipped lazing around shallow water. Plenty of larger species pass by Hawai'i, but tend to prefer the deeper waters in the channels.

DOLPHINS

Spinner dolphins are frequently seen in large schools (about 200). They swim as small family groups within these schools, and often swim fast, leaping from the water, spinning in the air. They tend to hang out in certain locations, so you can search them out if you like.

Bottlenose dolphins often approach fast-moving boats, and it is a great thrill to watch them race along just next to the bow of your boat, jumping in and out of the water with grace and easy speed.

Beaked and spotted dolphins are also commonly seen in Hawai'i.

SEA TURTLES

Common at many Hawai'ian reefs, though they usually stay away from humans. Some do seem nearly tame— or at least unconcerned about snorkelers.

Sea turtles are often seen in pairs. Larger specimens (often seen at Kahalu'u Beach) might be more than 100 years old, and tend to be docile and unafraid. You'll often see them resting on the bottom in about ten to twenty feet of water during the day. They will let you swim as close as you like, but if you hover over them, they might be afraid to come up for air. Just before dusk, they often hunt for food along the coast.

Do not disturb these graceful creatures, so that they can remain unafraid to swim among snorkelers. In Hawai'i it is against the law to touch or harass these magnificent animals.

WHALES

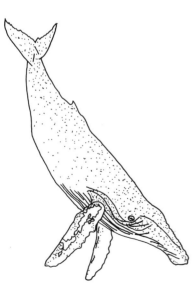

Humpback whales migrate here to breed in winter, around early-December. Humpbacks come quite close to the coast, where you can watch whole families. They are so large that you can often easily see them spouting and breaching. If you bring binoculars, you can see them well from shore. Their great size never fails to impress, as does their fluid, seemingly effortless graceful movement in the water.

Weather

All islands have a windward side, which is wetter, and a leeward side which is drier. In Hawai'i, the northeast is windward and hence wet, and the southwest is leeward, or kona, and hence drier and sunnier. Waves from afar tend to arrive from the north in winter and from the south in summer, although this pattern changes often.

Hawai'i gets most of its rain in the winter. The most severe storms (called kona), however, come from the south and can even bring hurricanes in the summer. Temperatures tend to be very mild year-round, yet there is variety around Hawai'i on any day of the year. There are days when you could get a hot tan in Kona in the morning, drive up to chilly Volcanoes later, while it rains buckets in Hilo. Summer temperatures are five degrees F warmer than winter.

Evaporating moisture from the ocean forms clouds. As the clouds rise over the mountains, they cool, and the condensing moisture becomes rain. Hilo receives rain more than 300 days a year, while Kohala only gets about 9 inches.

Having lost most of their moisture in passing over the mountains, the clouds have little left for the leeward side—so it is in the rain shadow of the mountains. The leeward weather is therefore often sunny. Waikiki, Poipu, Ka'anapali, and Kona are all in rain shadows. On Hawai'i, if you get stuck with heavy rains in Hilo, just head for Kona to find the sun.

Changeable is the word for Hawai'i's weather—not just between areas, but also rapidly changeable in any given place. The trade winds blow about 90% of the time in the summer and about 50% in the winter. They tend to be stronger in the afternoon and are sometimes strong in Kohala and usually strong at South Point.

The windward or northeastern coasts have much more rain, wind and waves—something important to remember when snorkeling.

Christmas wrasse

Seasonal Changes

Hawai'i has much milder weather than the continental United States, yet it is has seasons you might call winter, spring and summer. At 20°N Latitude, there are nearly 2 1/2 hours more sun in midsummer than in midwinter, which is 21% more. But the thermal mass of the ocean keeps temperature swings quite moderate.

Winter is the cooler, wetter season. Cooler is a relative term, as the average high temperature in winter falls to a brisk 80° F, as opposed to a summer average high of 88° F. Water temperature in winter falls to around 77° F, and at times, wind, rain and cooler air temperatures can temper your desire to splash around in the water. Winter usually begins in mid-November, with the start of winter storms from the north-northwest. This is the start of the large wave season on the north coast. Winter tails off in mid-March.

Spring really is just the transition from winter to summer, and is marked by the end of winter storms in mid-March. Hours of sunshine go up, especially on the west, leeward side of the island. This can be a very pleasant time of year. Spring transitions into summer in May.

Summer begins in May, as the weather warms, and the rains slacken. Trade winds temper the heat and humidity almost all the time. This is prime sunning and play time. An occasional tropical storm or hurricane can come through, and swells can roll in from the south. The heat softens in October as summer draws to an end.

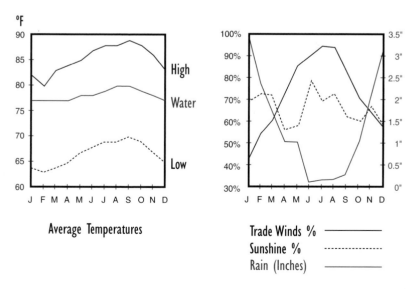

Average Temperatures

Trade Winds % ————
Sunshine % ------------
Rain (Inches) ————

Month by Month

JANUARY: This month offers an opportunity for the wettest weather all year. It's also one of the coolest. Large surf can often pound the north and west exposed beaches.

FEBRUARY: Just as cool, the surf continues to hit the north and west exposed beaches, although storms are a bit less frequent.

MARCH: The weather starts to improve with fewer storms, especially in the west.

APRIL: Spring arrives early, so warm weather begins during this month.

MAY: Summer is already arriving—especially in the south and west. This tends to be a trouble-free month.

JUNE: This offers very warm and dry weather with plenty of sun. Fortunately the winds blow nearly every day.

JULY: Much the same as June, except that storms in the South Pacific begin at this time. They hit beaches exposed to the south.

AUGUST: Another warm month, occasional big waves can hit the southern exposed beaches.

SEPTEMBER: This last month of summer can sometimes be the hottest and most humid. Hurricanes can strike Hawai'i, and are most common this month. Most will miss the islands, but bring muggy weather. Iniki, however, brought widespread damage to Kaua'i.

OCTOBER: Milder weather begins this month with the start of storms arriving from the north.

NOVEMBER: Sometimes the first real winter storms arrive and they can be somewhat cool.

DECEMBER: This is winter with frequent storms and wind bringing big waves to the exposed northern and western beaches. However, even this month can be clear and warm between storms.

Coolest month:	February
Hottest month:	September
Rainiest month:	January
Driest month:	June
Coolest water:	December-April
Warmest water:	August-September

Tides

Tides are very slight in Hawai'i, with the average difference between high and low only 2-3 feet max. It's a good idea to know which way the tide is going because tidal flow does affect the currents. If the tide is going out, you might want to avoid snorkeling in places where water is already shallow (like Puako) or where currents tend to sweep out of a bay, often the center, or a gap in the reef (see Understanding Waves, page 27).

Water Temperature

On the surface, the water in Hawai'i averages a low of about 77° F (25° C) in March to a high of about 80° F (27° C) in September. Sheltered bays can be a bit warmer, while deeper or rough water can be surprisingly cool. The Big Island, being furthest south, can be warmer. If you happen to be slender, no longer young, or from a moderate climate, winter seas can seem cooler than you like—especially if you like to snorkel for hours.

Hurricanes

Summer is hurricane season, but it is also the time when weather is typically excellent. While the storms don't last long, they can be terribly destructive. Hurricanes can bring amazingly heavy rain and winds to all the islands. Any of the islands could receive a direct hit, which happened when Hurricanes Ewa and Iniki clobbered Kaua'i.

Tsunamis

Huge waves can be triggered by earthquakes either in the islands or far across the Pacific. They've hit Hawai'i numerous times, more often from the north. Some very destructive tsunamis have hit and swept over the lowest land. Depending on the exact direction, they can directly hit a valley and really wipe it out and rinse it clean. It is probably better to not be there when this happens, unless you're one great surfer dude. Tsunami waves are often spaced as far as fifteen minutes apart.

Currently there's usually plenty of warning and authorities prefer to warn of every possible tsunami just to be safe. It doesn't pay to ignore warnings just because the sea appears calm. If a major earthquake strikes while you're visiting, it's a good idea to head rapidly for high ground. Leave bays or valleys which can act to funnel the effects of a large wave. The worst tsunamis can hit several times—with a space of about fifteen minutes between waves.

Geology

To understand what's happening today in Hawai'i, begin by casting your thoughts back about 30 million years. At that time lava was bubbling out in the middle of the Pacific about 20,000' below the ocean surface, due to a volcanic hot spot directly underneath. Molten rock pushing up through the ocean floor formed volcanoes under the sea. Lava built up, layer after layer, until it finally reached the surface to form the first island.

As the volcanoes grew, the weight of these early islands gradually caused them to sink down again, forming atolls. The Pacific Plate drifted northwest, while the hot spot remained stationary. A long string of more than 30 islands were formed, stretching from Midway Island to the southeast 1600 miles all the way to the Big Island. Another island is already rising in the sea close to the southeast coast of the Big Island. Loihi Sea Mount is now just 3000' under the surface, and will probably join the Big Island as it emerges. Lava flowing into the sea from Kilauea has been intermittently building the Big Island daily toward Loihi.

Most of the current above-water mass is now concentrated in eight islands. Kaua'i, about 5 million years old, is the oldest of these, while the Big Island is less than 1 million years old. As these islands drift approximately 4 inches northwest each year, the lava conduits to their volcanoes bend until new conduits are formed. Eventually, the next volcano in the chain takes over the job of releasing the unremitting pressure from pools of magma far below.

And a Little Natural History, Too

When each underground mountain emerges from the sea, coral larvae begin to establish their new homes on the volcanic rocks around the base. Stony coral is one of the first ocean creatures to reach and become established on a new island.

These larvae travel island by island—originally coming in a very round-about fashion on the currents from the ancient reefs surrounding Indonesia. Once they became established, it was easier for new larvae to reach the next nearby island. The reef begins as a fringe around the island. Each polyp of coral secretes a skeleton of calcium carbonate. Gradually the colony grows large enough to provide a home for other plants and animals.

All of the major Hawai'ian islands now have fringing reefs around much of the shore. The Big Island, still in formation, is not yet fully surrounded by reef. As the islands grow, get heavy and gradually sink, the reef changes as well. The older islands of Kaua'i and O'ahu have very old coral reef deposits on land—remnants of a time when the sea level was higher.

Coral reefs are made up of coral animals and algae growing on top of the dead skeletons of former creatures. In search of sunlight, they continue to grow upward toward the light, as they need to stay within 150 feet of the surface of the sea.

The outside of a reef grows faster than the inner surface, so eventually a lagoon forms between the reef and the land. The reef is then called a barrier reef, limited examples of which can be found in Kaua'i and O'ahu.

Since the currents in Hawai'i come mainly from Japan rather than the warmer south Pacific, they bring less variety of reef life. Larvae need to survive long enough to reach an island and establish themselves before sending out the next generation, so it's helpful to have stepping-stone islands in order to have greater variety. Most will not survive long enough to cross the large open Pacific ocean.

Tahiti has a much greater variety of coral because of the stepping-stone islands leading all the way from Southeast Asia. Hawai'i, in contrast, is one of the most isolated island groups in the world. It also has somewhat cooler water and less sunlight than Tahiti, making it less hospitable to some species. This isolation has kept all species of plant and animal life rather limited, and also encouraged the evolution of unique species found only in Hawai'i. These unique species are referred to as endemic. They give Hawai'i a special character—both above and below the water. More than 30% of the fish seen here are found nowhere else in the world. The cooler water in Hawai'i has protected the island's reefs from coral bleaching, which has caused so much damage to much of the earth's reefs.

For millions of years the Hawai'ian Islands had no plants or animals in spite of the rich soil, due to their 2000-mile isolation from other large land masses. When plants and animals finally did arrive, they found little competition and a superb climate. The lack of competition meant plants did not require thorns or other protective features. Some plants and animals found such a perfect environment that they thrived. Before man arrived, Hawai'i had no fruits or vegetables. The Polynesians, and later arrivals, changed this environment enormously by their imports and cultivation.

Most of the "exotic" plants that you may think of as quintessentially Hawai'ian were brought by man (mango, papaya, pineapple, orchid, ginger, hibiscus). Koa and ohia, on the other hand, pre-date man's arrival. Ohia is often the first to grow on lava flows and has produced much of the Hawai'ian rain forest.

Unfortunately, most of the rain forest has already been destroyed by animals brought by man (such as cattle and goats) or cleared to provide land for sugar production. Sugar and pineapple production now appear to be on the way out, a casualty of world economics. Tourism has now replaced these crops, but takes its own severe toll on the fragile islands of Hawai'i.

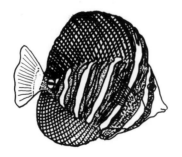

sailfin tang

Reef Development

Hawai'ian reefs have weathered at least four major changes in the distant past. Many land-based plants and animals also became extinct during these changes and others took their place. Current reefs are composed mostly of shallow water reef coral. They incorporate algae in their structure, and the algae is dependent on photosynthesis.

Different plants and animals live in the varied locations on the reef depending primarily on wave action. Species living on the outer edge of the reef are skilled at surviving strong waves and currents. Lagoon species don't have to endure this, so the lagoon supports more delicate life.

Hawai'i has a number of strikingly different reef habitats—each with its own story to tell. Where the water is rough, cauliflower coral dominates. The more delicate finger coral grows only in the calm lagoon areas. Large boulders are common in the open waters, especially where wave action is heaviest, and they support entirely different creatures. Caves, caverns and old lava tubes are abundant here. Steep drop-offs serve as an upwelling source of plankton-rich water, which attracts many larger creatures to feed. Sandy habitat is found scattered around the Big Island. A thriving reef is developing around much of the island.

Language

English is now the official language of the islands of Hawai'i—except for the island of Ni'ihau. However, most place names and lots of slang are Hawai'ian, so it's helpful to at least be able to pronounce Hawai'ian enough to be understood. It's a very straight-forward phonetic language—each letter usually pronounced just one way. The long place names aren't nearly so daunting when you've learned the system.

All syllables begin with a consonant that is followed by at least one vowel. When the missionaries attempted to write this spoken language, they used only seven consonants (h,k,l,m,n,p,w) and five vowels (a,e,i,o,u). More recently, in an effort to help outsiders pronounce Hawai'ian, the glottal stop (called an 'okina) has been added—marked by '. For example, in Hawai'i, the ' is used to indicate that each i should be pronounced separately: Ha-wai-i, rather than Ha-waii.

A horizontal line (called a macron) is sometimes placed over vowels to be given a longer duration. Nene, for example, is "Naay-Naay". Unfortunately, our typeface doesn't allow macrons. Each and every letter is pronounced in Hawai'ian, except for a few vowel combinations. However, locals often shorten names a bit, so listen carefully to the way natives pronounce a name. Another addition to the language is a form of pidgin, which served to ease the difficulties of having multiple languages spoken. Laborers were brought in speaking Japanese, Mandarin, Cantonese, Portuguese, English, as well as other languages, and they had to be able to work together. Pidgin evolved as an ad hoc, but surprisingly effective way to communicate, and much of it survives in slang and common usage today.

Pronunciation

Consonants are pronounced the same as in English, except that the W sometimes sounds more like a V when it appears in the middle of a word. Vowels are pronounced as follows:

a = long as in father
e = short as in den, or long as the ay in say
i = long as the ee in sea
o = round as in no
u = round as the ou in you

When vowels are joined (as they often are), pronounce each, with slightly more emphasis on the first one. This varies with local usage.

Commonly Used Vocabulary and Place Names

'a'a = rough lava (of Hawai'ian origin, now used worldwide)
'ahi = tuna, especially yellowfin (albacore) tuna
ahupua'a = land division in pie shape from mountain to sea
ali'i = chief
aloha = hello, goodbye, expressing affection
haole = foreigner (now usually meaning a white person)
heiau = temple, religious platform
hula = native Hawai'ian dance
humuhumunukunukuapua'a = trigger fish that is Hawai'ian state fish
imu = pit for steaming food over hot stones
kahuna = powerful priest
kai = sea
kama'aina = long-time resident of the islands
kane = male
kapu = taboo
ko'ala = barbequed
kokua = help
kona = leeward, or away from the direction of the wind
kukui = candlenut (state tree)
lei = garland of flowers, shells, etc. given as a symbol of affection
lu'au = Hawai'ian traditional feast, including roast pork and poi
mahalo = thanks; admiration, praise, respect
mahimahi = dolphinfish (not a dolphin)
makai = on the seaside, towards the sea, or in that direction
malihini = recent arrival to the islands, tourist, stranger
mana = power coming from the spirit world
mano = shark
mauka = upland, towards the mountains
mauna = mountain, peak
menehune = little people of legend, here before the Polynesians
moana = ocean
nene = Hawai'ian state bird
niu = coconut
ohana = extended family
ono = the best, delicious, savory; to relish or crave
pahoehoe = lava that has a smooth texture (used worldwide)
paka lolo = marijuana
pali = cliff
pupu = appetizer, snack
taro (Polynesian word) = starchy root plant used to make poi
wahine = female
wai = fresh water
wana = sea urchin

Often Heard Myths

- **"You'll probably never see a shark."**

  If you snorkel often, you probably will see one occasionally, a reef shark, not a Great White or Tiger Shark. Most sharks aren't interested in you for dinner. If you look at actual statistics, your time is better spent worrying about lightning.

- **"Barracudas are harmless to humans."**

  Perhaps some are quite innocuous, but others have bitten off fingers or hands. The Great Barracuda has been involved in the majority of cases we've read. Don't worry about one that has been hanging out in front of a hotel for years, but you may not want to crowd them either. I'd be even more cautious about eating one for dinner, because they are a definite, major cause of ciguatera "fish poisoning". They are one of the best tasting fish, though, in our experience. Feeling lucky?

- **"Jewelry attracts barracuda bites."**

  I first heard this rumor from a 12-year-old, and it was later reinforced by numerous books. The idea is that the flash will fool a barracuda into attacking. However, we've never heard of a definite case of a woman losing an ear lobe this way, even though I see people swimming and diving with earrings all the time. The same goes for wedding bands. I keep mine on.

- **"The water in Hawai'i is too cold for comfort."**
  "The water is Hawai'i is as warm as bath water."

  It can be pretty cool, especially late winter, especially if you go in naked; but there is an alternative. Just wear a thin wetsuit and it will feel a lot like the Caribbean in summer. Or you can wait till late summer and give the water a chance to warm up. Don't expect bath-warm water in Hawaii in March.

- **"It rains all the time on the Big Island."**
  "The Big Island is too hot and sunny."
  "It's always windy at South Point."

  On the Big Island, you can have the climate of your choice. Don't believe everything you read in advertising literature (like hotel brochures) regarding perfect weather. It does vary, there are seasons, and location matters. It just depends on your personal preferences. You may hit a patch of rain, but it seldom lasts for long. The typical weather report for Kona is: Tonight—fair; Tomorrow, mostly sunny; for the weekend, sunny except for some upslope clouds in the afternoon.The drama of weather is part of the charm of the tropics—enjoy it as it is, rather than expecting it to be exactly as you want.

- **"Octopuses only come out at night."**

Some types are nocturnal, some not. We've seen lots in Hawai'i quite active during the day. The hard part is spotting them! Pay your dues, look sharp, and you'll see one eventually. Broad inner lagoons with rubble are an excellent place to look.

- **"The Big Island is getting too crowded and commercial."**

While there is certainly no problem buying a T-shirt in town or finding sun-worshippers on the beaches, there are plenty of spectacular sites to snorkel that are completely uncrowded. As long as you have a car, it's easy to drive to delightful and secluded locations—usually within half an hour from your hotel or condo. Hiking on the Big Island can take you completely away from civilization as you know it, but a good map (such as ours) can lead you to some lovely snorkeling sites as well as romantic vistas to enjoy the sunset and the view of neighboring islands.

- **"The food is too expensive."**

Restaurant food is not inexpensive, but it also costs no more than in most major urban areas. In a grocery store, certain items cost a fair amount more, especially fresh produce that must be flown in. But there are solutions. Rent a condo, pick up a trunk-load of staples at the market as you leave the airport, and check out the great variety of foods at the local grocery with Hawai'ian specialties. Try the hearty Hawai'ian "plate lunch", which is inexpensive and doesn't leave room for a full dinner. Be sure to check out the Kona coffee, local fresh fruits, Maui onions, and ever-popular bakeries and ice cream vendors. There's no reason to go hungry in Hawai'i.

Snorkeling the Internet

We figure some of you are really wired. Brought your laptop along to poolside just for fun? Just got one of those new SportsLaptops with the rubberized keyboard? Maybe you don't even have to get out of the water to log on the net, who knows?

We like speed, too, but book writing and publishing is still a slow business. You wouldn't believe how many long, hard hours we spend slaving away, snorkeling and researching, researching and snorkeling some more, in order to produce the little volume you're holding. Maybe a hundred hours of research gets distilled into one little page of maps and text. It makes me sweat just to think about it.

Oh, yeah, *some tough job*, I hear someone saying. We get no sympathy. But we have learned to live with that, and snorkel on. To enable the wired to get the latest corrections and additions between revisions, we've created **snorkelguides.com** We post links to Hawai'ian resources there, as well as updates to phone numbers, excursions, and many other goodies.

There are a lot of good resources on the Web, more every day. Check out our progress on other snorkeling guidebooks. Or you can find out how to order copies to send to all your friends. A great Christmas or birthday gift, a lot better than another pair of socks for good old Dad! Encourage healthy snorkeling!

We'd love to hear what you like or don't like about our books, and reports about your experiences snorkeling. If you've found a great snorkeling site anywhere in the world, let us know via e-mail if you can and we'll share some of our favorites, too. The Web is changing hourly, so the best way to get current links is to go to our Web page, and just click on them!

Warning: The Web is getting more and more commercial. It's a libertarian's dream, anarchic, free and open, unfettered and sometimes chaotic. The downside to this unregulated utopia: you can't tell whether someone has a hidden agenda, knows what they're talking about, or is just plain lying. Watch out! Remember to maintain a healthy skepticism as you surf the web. Many of the elaborate sites are commercial, so what seems to be an objective review might have been bought and paid for. Someone selling excursions may only list those that give them a big cut. Be streetwise as you enjoy the web, and you'll be OK.

Order Form

Snorkel Hawai'i books make great birthday or holiday gifts. Get that friend or loved one off their duff and off to Hawai'i to snorkel!

If you like Snorkel Hawai'i, and decide to give the other islands a try, we have some special deals available for repeat readers who buy more than one book at a time. Just make a photocopy of this order form, and mail it along with your check payable to:

Indigo Publications
920 Los Robles Avenue
Palo Alto, CA 94306

one title: $14.00

two titles: $25.00

three titles: $34.00

Please order the following:

Quantity   Title

_____   Snorkel Hawai'i: The Big Island

_____   Snorkel Kaua'i

_____   Snorkel Maui and Lana'i

_____   price subtotal for books

_____   sales tax (CA residents only)

$ 2.00   shipping charge

_____   total enclosed

ship to: _____

                  _____

                  _____

Index

About the Authors

Judy and Mel Malinowski love to snorkel in the warm oceans of the tropics.

This love has led them to embark on snorkeling and cultural adventures to 60-some countries from Anguilla to Zanzibar. Hawai'i keeps drawing them back to their second home on the sunny South Kohala coast.

Although they are certified Scuba divers, the lightness and freedom of snorkeling keeps it their favorite recreation.

Mel, Judy and their three children have hosted students and cultural exchange visitors from Bosnia, Brazil, China, Germany, Nepal, New Zealand, Serbia, and Turkey in their home, and helped hundreds of other families enrich their lives through cultural exchange.

Working with exchange students and traveling as much as their businesses allow has encouraged their interest in the study of languages from Chinese to Spanish.

Graduates of Stanford University, they live in Palo Alto, California.